Parenting With Purpose: Nurturing Children With ADHD

Barley Nicola

Published by Barley Nicola, 2024.

While every precaution has been taken in the preparation of this book, the publisher assumes no responsibility for errors or omissions, or for damages resulting from the use of the information contained herein.

PARENTING WITH PURPOSE: NURTURING CHILDREN WITH ADHD

First edition. March 30, 2024.

ISBN: 979-8224774111

Written by Barley Nicola.

Table of Contents

Chapter 1: Introduction

- What is ADHD?

Attention Deficit Hyperactivity Disorder (ADHD) is a neurodevelopmental disorder that affects individuals of all ages, but is most commonly diagnosed in childhood. It is characterized by a persistent pattern of inattention, hyperactivity, and impulsivity that can interfere with daily functioning and academic performance. While the exact cause of ADHD is not fully understood, research suggests that a combination of genetic, environmental, and neurological factors play a role in its development.

One of the key features of ADHD is inattention, which can manifest as difficulty focusing on tasks, being easily distracted, forgetfulness, and disorganization. This can impact an individual's ability to complete assignments, follow instructions, and stay on task. Hyperactivity is another core symptom of ADHD, characterized by excessive fidgeting, restlessness, and difficulty sitting still. Impulsivity, the third component of ADHD, involves acting without thinking, interrupting others, and making hasty decisions without considering the consequences.

ADHD is diagnosed based on a comprehensive evaluation by a qualified healthcare professional, typically a psychiatrist or psychologist. The diagnostic criteria for ADHD are outlined in the Diagnostic and Statistical Manual of Mental Disorders (DSM-5), which categorizes the disorder into three subtypes: predominantly inattentive presentation, predominantly hyperactive-impulsive presentation, and combined presentation. In order to meet the criteria for a diagnosis, symptoms must be present for at least six months and significantly impact daily functioning.

It is important to note that ADHD is not a one-size-fits-all condition, and symptoms can vary widely among individuals. While some may struggle primarily with inattention, others may exhibit more hyperactive or impulsive behaviors. Additionally, ADHD often co-occurs with other mental health conditions such as anxiety, depression, and learning disabilities. This can complicate the diagnostic process and may require a multidisciplinary approach to treatment.

Treatment for ADHD typically involves a combination of behavioral therapy, medication, and lifestyle modifications. Stimulant medications such as methylphenidate and amphetamine salts are commonly prescribed to help improve attention, reduce hyperactivity, and control impulsivity. These medications work by increasing the levels of dopamine and norepinephrine in the brain, resulting in improved focus and concentration. Non-stimulant medications, such as atomoxetine and guanfacine, may also be used in individuals who do not respond well to stimulants or have comorbid conditions that preclude their use.

In addition to medication, behavioral therapy is an essential component of ADHD treatment. Cognitive-behavioral therapy (CBT) and parent training programs can help individuals learn coping strategies, improve organizational skills, and develop effective communication techniques. These interventions can also address common comorbidities such as anxiety and depression, improving overall quality of life for individuals with ADHD.

Lifestyle modifications, such as regular exercise, adequate sleep, and a healthy diet, can also play a role in managing ADHD symptoms. Physical activity has been shown to improve attention and impulse control, while a balanced diet rich in vitamins, minerals, and omega-3 fatty acids can support cognitive function. Establishing a routine with clear expectations and structure can help individuals with ADHD stay organized and on track. While there is no cure for ADHD, early diagnosis and intervention can help individuals learn to manage their symptoms effectively. By implementing a comprehensive treatment plan that includes medication, behavioral therapy, and lifestyle modifications, individuals with ADHD can improve their attention, impulse control, and overall well-being. It is important to seek support from qualified healthcare professionals to create a personalized treatment plan that meets the unique needs of each individual with ADHD.

- Understanding the challenges faced by children with ADHD

Attention-deficit/hyperactivity disorder (ADHD) is a neurodevelopmental disorder that impacts individuals across the lifespan. However, it primarily manifests in childhood, with symptoms such as inattention, hyperactivity, and impulsivity. Children with ADHD may struggle academically, socially, and emotionally due to the challenges posed by the disorder. These challenges can have a significant impact on the overall well-being and functioning of children with ADHD, as well as their families and caregivers.

One of the primary challenges faced by children with ADHD is in the academic domain. Children with ADHD may have difficulty focusing on tasks, staying organized, and completing assignments on time. These challenges can lead to poor academic performance, lower self-esteem, and increased frustration for both the child and their teachers. Children with ADHD may also struggle with following instructions, listening attentively, and staying on task during classroom activities. As a result, they may require additional support and accommodations in order to effectively access the curriculum and succeed academically.

In addition to academic challenges, children with ADHD may also face difficulties in social situations. Due to their impulsivity and hyperactivity, children with ADHD may struggle to regulate their behaviors and emotions in social interactions. This can lead to misunderstandings, conflicts, and social isolation. Children with ADHD may have difficulty making and maintaining friendships, interpreting social cues, and understanding the perspectives of others. As a result, they may experience feelings of loneliness, rejection, and low self-esteem. It is important for parents, teachers, and other caregivers to provide social skills training and support to help children with ADHD navigate social situations effectively.

Emotional challenges are also common among children with ADHD. Due to their difficulties with attention, impulse control, and hyperactivity, children with ADHD may experience heightened levels of stress, frustration, and emotional dysregulation. They may struggle to cope with everyday challenges, setbacks, and transitions. Children with ADHD may also be more prone to mood swings, tantrums, and outbursts of anger or frustration. It is essential for parents, teachers, and mental health professionals to provide children with ADHD with strategies and support to help them manage their emotions effectively and develop healthy coping mechanisms.

Furthermore, children with ADHD may also experience challenges in the home environment. Parents of children with ADHD may feel overwhelmed, exhausted, and frustrated by the demands of caring for a child with ADHD. They may struggle to meet the unique needs of their child, while also balancing work, household responsibilities, and their own well-being. Siblings of children with ADHD may also experience feelings of resentment, jealousy, or neglect due to the focus and attention given to the child with ADHD. It is important for parents and families to access support services, resources, and counseling to help them navigate the challenges of raising a child with ADHD and promote a positive and supportive family environment. It is essential for parents, teachers, healthcare professionals, and communities to understand and address these challenges in order to support the well-being and development of children with ADHD. By providing appropriate interventions, accommodations, and support, children with ADHD can thrive and succeed in all areas of their lives. With the right resources and strategies in place, children with ADHD can overcome the challenges posed by their disorder and reach their full potential.

- Importance of effective parenting strategies for children with ADHD

Parenting a child with ADHD can be a challenging and overwhelming task. Children with ADHD often struggle with impulsivity, inattention, hyperactivity, and difficulty staying focused. As a result, they may have trouble with schoolwork, social interactions, and behavior management. Effective parenting strategies are crucial in helping these children thrive and succeed in all areas of their life.

One of the most important aspects of effective parenting for children with ADHD is establishing clear and consistent routines. Children with ADHD thrive on structure and predictability, so having a daily routine in place can help them stay organized and manage their time more effectively. This can involve setting specific times for meals, homework, bedtime, and other activities, as well as providing reminders and cues to help them stay on track.

Another key parenting strategy for children with ADHD is setting clear expectations and boundaries. Children with ADHD often have trouble regulating their behavior and may act impulsively or engage in disruptive behaviors. By setting clear expectations and boundaries, parents can help their child understand what is expected of them and what behaviors are appropriate. This can include establishing rules and consequences for misbehavior, as well as providing positive reinforcement for good behavior.

In addition to setting clear routines and expectations, it is also important for parents to provide their child with plenty of opportunities for physical activity and exercise. Children with ADHD often have high levels of energy and may struggle to sit still for long periods of time. By encouraging them to engage in regular physical activity, parents can help their child burn off excess energy and improve their focus and concentration.

Parenting a child with ADHD also requires a high level of patience and understanding. Children with ADHD may have trouble following directions, completing tasks, and controlling their impulses, which can be frustrating for both the child and the parent. It is important for parents to remain calm and patient, and to avoid getting frustrated or angry when their child struggles. By providing emotional support and encouragement, parents can help their child build confidence and develop the skills they need to succeed.

Furthermore, it is essential for parents of children with ADHD to educate themselves about the disorder and its symptoms. By learning more about ADHD, parents can gain a better understanding of their child's behavior and how to best support them. This may involve reading books, attending support groups, or seeking guidance from mental health professionals. By educating themselves about ADHD, parents can become better equipped to help their child navigate the challenges they face. By establishing clear routines, setting expectations and boundaries, providing opportunities for physical activity, practicing patience and understanding, and educating themselves about the disorder, parents can help their child reach their full potential. While parenting a child with ADHD may be challenging at times, with the right approach and support, children with ADHD can lead happy, healthy, and successful lives.

Chapter 2: Recognizing ADHD Symptoms

- Common symptoms of ADHD in children

Attention-deficit/hyperactivity disorder (ADHD) is a neurodevelopmental disorder that affects children and can persist into adulthood. It is characterized by a persistent pattern of inattention and/or hyperactivity-impulsivity that interferes with daily functioning or development. While the exact causes of ADHD are not fully understood, research suggests that a combination of genetic, environmental, and neurological factors play a role in its development. Diagnosis of ADHD in children is typically based on a thorough evaluation of symptoms, including a detailed history of behavior in various settings such as school and home.

One of the most common symptoms of ADHD in children is inattention. Children with ADHD often have difficulty staying focused on tasks and may become easily distracted by external stimuli. They may struggle to follow instructions or complete assignments, leading to poor academic performance and frustration. Inattentive symptoms of ADHD may also manifest in forgetfulness, disorganization, and difficulty with time management. These challenges can impact a child's ability to function effectively in school and social settings, leading to feelings of frustration and low self-esteem.

Another key symptom of ADHD in children is hyperactivity. Children with ADHD may exhibit excessive restlessness, impulsivity, and a constant need for movement. They may have difficulty sitting still, waiting their turn, or engaging in quiet activities. Hyperactive symptoms of ADHD can be disruptive in classroom settings and may lead to conflicts with teachers and peers. Children with ADHD may also engage in risky behaviors or have difficulty regulating their emotions, leading to impulsivity and outbursts of anger.

In addition to inattention and hyperactivity, children with ADHD may also exhibit symptoms of impulsivity. Impulsivity in children with ADHD can manifest in a variety of ways, including interrupting others, blurting out answers, and acting without considering the consequences of their actions. Children with ADHD may have difficulty regulating their impulses, leading to challenges in social interactions and decision-making. Impulsive behaviors can also contribute to difficulties in self-control and may impact a child's ability to form and maintain relationships with peers.

It is important to recognize that symptoms of ADHD can vary among children and may present differently based on a child's age, gender, and individual characteristics. Some children with ADHD may predominantly exhibit symptoms of inattention, while others may display more hyperactive or impulsive behaviors. In some cases, symptoms of ADHD may not be immediately noticeable or may be mistaken for other conditions, such as anxiety or depression. As a result, a comprehensive evaluation by a qualified healthcare professional is essential for accurate diagnosis and treatment of ADHD in children.

Early identification and intervention for ADHD in children are critical for improving long-term outcomes and helping children reach their full potential. Effective treatment for ADHD typically involves a combination of behavioral therapy, medication, and parental support. Behavioral therapy can help children learn coping strategies to manage their symptoms and improve their attention, organization, and impulse control. Medication, such as stimulant medications or non-stimulants, may also be prescribed to help control symptoms of ADHD and improve focus and impulse control. Common symptoms of ADHD in children include inattention, hyperactivity, and impulsivity, which can impact a child's academic performance, social interactions, and emotional well-being. Early recognition and intervention are essential for supporting children with ADHD and promoting positive outcomes. With appropriate diagnosis and treatment, children with ADHD can learn to manage their symptoms and thrive in school and social settings. It is important for parents, educators, and healthcare professionals to work together to provide comprehensive support for children with ADHD and help them reach their full potential.

- Different types of ADHD

Attention-deficit/hyperactivity disorder (ADHD) is a neurodevelopmental disorder that affects both children and adults. It is characterized by a persistent pattern of inattention, hyperactivity, and impulsivity that can interfere with daily functioning and social interactions. There are three main types of ADHD: inattentive type, hyperactive-impulsive type, and combined type. Each type has its own unique set of symptoms and challenges.

The inattentive type of ADHD is characterized by difficulties with attention to detail, organization, and staying focused on tasks. Individuals with this type may struggle to follow instructions, complete tasks, and remember details. They may appear forgetful, disorganized, and easily distracted. This type of ADHD is more common in girls and may not be as easily identified as the hyperactive-impulsive type. It is important for parents and teachers to be aware of the symptoms of inattentive ADHD so that appropriate interventions and support can be provided.

The hyperactive-impulsive type of ADHD is characterized by excessive physical activity, fidgeting, and impulsivity. Individuals with this type may have difficulty sitting still, waiting their turn, and controlling their impulses. They may interrupt others, talk excessively, and have difficulty with self-regulation. This type of ADHD is more common in boys and is often more easily recognized by parents and teachers. It is important for individuals with hyperactive-impulsive ADHD to receive appropriate support and guidance to help them manage their symptoms and maximize their potential.

The combined type of ADHD is characterized by a combination of symptoms from both the inattentive and hyperactive-impulsive types. Individuals with this type may struggle with attention, organization, impulsivity, and hyperactivity. They may have difficulty in multiple areas of life, including school, work, and relationships. It is important for individuals with combined type ADHD to receive comprehensive assessment and treatment to address their unique needs and challenges. By understanding the different types of ADHD and how they present, parents, teachers, and mental health professionals can better support individuals with this disorder and help them thrive.

In addition to the three main types of ADHD, there are also subtypes that may be present in some individuals. These subtypes include sluggish cognitive tempo (SCT), which is characterized by daydreaming, slow processing speed, and cognitive difficulties; and ADHD predominantly inattentive presentation (ADHD-PI), which is similar to the inattentive type but may be less severe. It is important for clinicians to carefully assess individuals with ADHD to determine the most appropriate diagnosis and treatment plan. By recognizing the different types and subtypes of ADHD, clinicians can tailor interventions to meet the unique needs of each individual and improve outcomes. By understanding the different types and subtypes of ADHD, clinicians, parents, and teachers can better identify and support individuals with this disorder. Through early identification, comprehensive assessment, and appropriate interventions, individuals with ADHD can learn to manage their symptoms, improve their functioning, and thrive in all areas of life. It is essential for all stakeholders to work together to ensure that individuals with ADHD receive the support and care they need to reach their full potential.

- The importance of early detection and diagnosis

Early detection and diagnosis are crucial components in the successful management of various medical conditions. By identifying a disease or disorder in its early stages, healthcare providers have the opportunity to initiate treatment promptly and potentially prevent further complications. This proactive approach can lead to better outcomes for patients and may even save lives in some cases. In this essay, we will explore the importance of early detection and diagnosis, highlighting the benefits it offers to both individuals and the healthcare system as a whole.

One of the key advantages of early detection and diagnosis is the ability to intervene at a stage when treatment is most effective. Many medical conditions, such as cancer and cardiovascular disease, are more easily managed when detected early. For example, in the case of cancer, early detection can significantly increase the likelihood of successful treatment and improve the overall prognosis for patients. By identifying cancerous cells before they have had a chance to spread, healthcare providers can offer more targeted and less aggressive treatment options, leading to better outcomes and a higher quality of life for patients.

Additionally, early detection and diagnosis can help to reduce the burden on the healthcare system by decreasing the need for costly and resource-intensive interventions. When conditions are identified at an early stage, healthcare providers can implement less invasive and less expensive treatment options, which can ultimately save both time and money. By avoiding more complex and expensive procedures, early detection and diagnosis can help to alleviate the strain on healthcare resources and ensure that limited resources are allocated more efficiently.

Furthermore, early detection and diagnosis can empower individuals to take control of their own health and make informed decisions about their care. By identifying medical conditions early, patients have the opportunity to educate themselves about their condition and participate actively in their treatment plan. This can lead to improved adherence to treatment regimens and better overall health outcomes. Additionally, early detection and diagnosis can provide patients with a sense of reassurance and peace of mind, knowing that their condition is being closely monitored and managed by healthcare professionals. By identifying diseases and disorders early, healthcare providers have the opportunity to initiate treatment promptly, potentially prevent further complications, and improve outcomes for patients. Early detection and diagnosis also help to reduce the burden on the healthcare system, empower individuals to take control of their health, and promote better overall health outcomes. It is essential for healthcare providers and individuals alike to recognize the importance of early detection and diagnosis and work collaboratively to ensure that medical conditions are identified and managed effectively.

Chapter 3: Creating a Supportive Environment

- Tips for creating a structured and organized home environment

Creating a structured and organized home environment is essential for maintaining a sense of calm and efficiency in your daily life. A cluttered and disorganized home can lead to increased stress, wasted time, and decreased productivity. By implementing some simple tips and strategies, you can create a space that is both functional and aesthetically pleasing.

One of the first steps in creating a structured and organized home environment is to declutter your space. Begin by going through each room in your home and identifying items that you no longer use or need. Organize your belongings into three categories: keep, donate, and discard. Be ruthless in your decluttering efforts and don't be afraid to let go of items that no longer serve a purpose in your life. Once you have decluttered your space, you will be able to better organize the items that you do choose to keep.

Once you have decluttered your home, it's time to organize the items that you have chosen to keep. Invest in storage solutions such as bins, baskets, shelves, and storage containers to help keep your belongings organized and easily accessible. Consider utilizing labels or color-coding systems to help you easily locate items when you need them. Create designated spaces for items such as keys, mail, shoes, and coats to prevent clutter from accumulating in common areas.

Create a daily cleaning routine to help maintain a structured and organized home environment. Set aside time each day to do small tasks such as wiping down countertops, putting away laundry, and tidying up common areas. By staying on top of these tasks on a daily basis, you can prevent clutter from accumulating and maintain a clean and organized home. Additionally, schedule regular deep cleaning sessions to tackle larger tasks such as dusting, vacuuming, and organizing closets. By staying consistent with your cleaning routine, you can create a structured and organized home environment that is easy to maintain.

Consider implementing a daily schedule or routine to help you stay on track and maintain a sense of order in your home. Create a to-do list each day with tasks that need to be completed, such as meal preparation, chores, and errands. Prioritize your tasks and allocate specific time blocks for each one to help you stay focused and efficient. By following a daily schedule, you can avoid feeling overwhelmed by tasks and ensure that everything gets done in a timely manner. Additionally, consider incorporating relaxation and self-care activities into your daily routine to help you recharge and maintain a healthy work-life balance.

Create designated workspaces in your home to help you stay organized and focused on tasks. Whether you work from home or simply need a space to pay bills or do paperwork, having a designated workspace can help you separate work from leisure. Choose a quiet and well-lit area in your home to set up a desk or table with all of the necessary supplies and equipment. Keep your workspace clutter-free and organized, and make sure that it is a comfortable and inviting environment that allows you to be productive. By creating designated workspaces in your home, you can maintain a structured and organized environment that is conducive to getting things done. By decluttering your space, organizing your belongings, establishing a cleaning routine, following a daily schedule, and creating designated workspaces, you can create a home environment that is functional, aesthetically pleasing, and conducive to productivity. Implementing these tips and strategies will help you create a structured and organized home environment that promotes a sense of well-being and happiness.

- Strategies for minimizing distractions in the home

In today's fast-paced and technology-driven world, distractions are everywhere, especially in the comfort of our own homes. With the rise of smartphones, social media, streaming services, and constant notifications, it can be challenging to stay focused and productive. However, there are strategies that can help minimize distractions and create a more conducive environment for work or study.

One effective strategy for minimizing distractions in the home is to designate a specific workspace. This could be a separate room, a corner of a room, or even just a specific desk or table. Having a dedicated workspace sends a signal to your brain that it is time to focus and work. It also helps create a physical barrier between your work or study area and other areas of the home, reducing the temptation to wander or get sidetracked.

Another strategy is to set specific work hours and stick to a routine. By establishing a schedule and routine, you can create a sense of structure and predictability in your day. This can help reduce the likelihood of getting distracted by other tasks or activities that may seem more appealing in the moment. It can also help you prioritize your work and allocate your time more effectively.

In addition to setting a schedule, it is important to set specific goals and objectives for each work session. By breaking down tasks into smaller, manageable chunks and setting clear objectives, you can stay focused and motivated. This can also help you track your progress and stay on track, reducing the likelihood of getting distracted or feeling overwhelmed.

One common source of distractions in the home is technology. While technology has revolutionized the way we work and communicate, it can also be a major source of distraction. One effective strategy for minimizing distractions is to establish boundaries with technology. This could include setting specific times for checking email or social media, turning off notifications, or even using apps or tools to block distracting websites during work or study sessions.

Another strategy for minimizing distractions is to create a quiet and clutter-free environment. Clutter and noise can be major distractions, making it difficult to focus and concentrate. By clearing your workspace of unnecessary items, organizing your surroundings, and minimizing noise distractions, you can create a more peaceful and conducive environment for work or study.

It is also important to take regular breaks and incorporate physical activity into your daily routine. Taking short breaks throughout the day can help refresh your mind and body, helping you stay focused and productive. Physical activity can also help reduce stress and improve cognitive function, making it easier to stay on task and minimize distractions.

In a nutshell, it is important to practice self-discipline and develop healthy habits. This could include setting boundaries with family members or roommates, establishing a bedtime routine, and creating a balance between work, leisure, and self-care. By prioritizing your well-being and creating healthy habits, you can create a more sustainable and productive work environment, minimizing distractions and maximizing your potential. By implementing strategies such as creating a dedicated workspace, setting a schedule and routine, establishing boundaries with technology, creating a quiet and clutter-free environment, taking regular breaks, and practicing self-discipline, you can create a more conducive environment for work or study. By prioritizing your focus and well-being, you can create a more sustainable and productive work environment, minimizing distractions and maximizing your potential.

- Importance of developing routines and schedules

Developing routines and schedules is crucial for maintaining productivity, achieving goals, and reducing stress in our daily lives. By establishing a structured plan for our day-to-day activities, we can increase our efficiency and effectiveness in completing tasks and meeting deadlines. Routines provide a sense of stability and predictability, allowing us to focus our energy on important tasks without being overwhelmed by decision-making and constant distractions. They also help us form good habits and break bad ones, leading to improved overall well-being and success in both personal and professional aspects of life.

One of the key benefits of developing routines and schedules is the ability to prioritize tasks and manage time effectively. By allocating specific time slots for different activities, we can ensure that important tasks are completed in a timely manner and that we are not wasting time on unproductive or unnecessary activities. This helps us stay organized and focused, enabling us to make the most of our day and achieve our goals more efficiently. Additionally, having a routine allows us to establish a work-life balance, ensuring that we have dedicated time for work, relaxation, and social activities.

Another important aspect of routines and schedules is their role in reducing stress and anxiety. When we have a clear plan for our day, we can avoid feeling overwhelmed by the demands of our daily responsibilities. Knowing what to expect and having a structured routine in place helps us manage our time more effectively and reduce the uncertainty and chaos that often lead to stress. By establishing consistent routines, we can create a sense of stability and control in our lives, which can significantly improve our mental and emotional well-being.

Furthermore, routines and schedules help us develop discipline and self-control, which are essential qualities for achieving success in any endeavor. By following a set routine, we can cultivate a sense of commitment and determination, as well as develop the ability to stick to our plans and goals despite obstacles and challenges. This helps us build resilience and perseverance, enabling us to stay focused and motivated in pursuit of our objectives. In this way, routines and schedules not only improve our productivity but also foster personal growth and development, leading to long-term success and fulfillment.

Additionally, developing routines and schedules can improve our overall health and well-being. By incorporating regular exercise, healthy eating habits, and self-care activities into our daily routine, we can enhance our physical and mental health. Routines help us establish healthy habits that support our well-being, such as getting an adequate amount of sleep, staying hydrated, and practicing mindfulness. By making these activities a regular part of our daily routine, we can improve our overall quality of life and reduce the risk of chronic health problems. By establishing structured plans for our daily activities, we can increase our productivity, reduce stress, and achieve our goals more effectively. Routines provide a sense of stability and predictability, enabling us to prioritize tasks, manage time, and maintain a healthy work-life balance. They also help us develop discipline and self-control, fostering personal growth and resilience in the face of challenges. By incorporating healthy habits into our routines, we can improve our overall health and well-being, leading to a happier and more fulfilling life. Therefore, it is important to prioritize the development of routines and schedules in order to maximize our potential and achieve long-term success.

Chapter 4: Positive Parenting Techniques

- Strategies for improving communication with children with ADHD

ADHD, or Attention-Deficit/Hyperactivity Disorder, is a neurodevelopmental disorder that can present challenges in communication for children affected by it. Effective communication with children with ADHD is crucial for their academic, social, and emotional development. By employing specific strategies and techniques tailored to their unique needs, parents, educators, and other caregivers can help children with ADHD improve their communication skills and reach their full potential.

One important strategy for improving communication with children with ADHD is using clear and concise language. Children with ADHD often have difficulty processing and retaining complex information. By keeping instructions and explanations simple and straightforward, caregivers can help these children better understand and respond to what is being communicated. It can be helpful to break down tasks or directions into smaller, manageable steps, and to provide clear and specific feedback on their progress.

Another effective strategy is to provide structure and routine in communication. Children with ADHD can benefit from having predictable routines and clear expectations. By establishing consistent communication patterns and routines, caregivers can help children with ADHD feel more secure and focused. This can include using visual aids, such as charts or schedules, to help children understand and remember important information. Setting clear boundaries and expectations can also help children with ADHD navigate social interactions and communication more effectively.

Active listening is a crucial skill in improving communication with children with ADHD. Children with ADHD may struggle to focus or stay engaged in conversations, so it is important for caregivers to show genuine interest and attention when communicating with them. This can involve maintaining eye contact, nodding or affirming their statements, and asking open-ended questions to encourage them to express themselves. By actively listening and acknowledging their thoughts and feelings, caregivers can build trust and establish a positive communication dynamic with children with ADHD.

Incorporating movement and physical activity into communication can also be beneficial for children with ADHD. Children with ADHD often have excess energy and may struggle to sit still during conversations or activities. Allowing them to move around or engage in physical activities while communicating can help them stay focused and engaged. This can involve incorporating movement breaks, using hands-on activities or manipulatives, or engaging in sensory play to enhance communication and learning experiences for children with ADHD.

Collaborating with teachers, therapists, and other professionals can also be an effective strategy for improving communication with children with ADHD. These professionals can offer valuable insights, strategies, and resources to support the communication needs of children with ADHD. By working together as a team, caregivers can ensure that children with ADHD receive the necessary support and accommodations to thrive academically, socially, and emotionally. Regular communication and collaboration can help caregivers and professionals share information, track progress, and make informed decisions to meet the needs of children with ADHD. By employing strategies such as using clear language, providing structure and routine, practicing active listening, incorporating movement and physical activity, and collaborating with professionals, caregivers can help children with ADHD develop their communication skills and reach their full potential. With the right support and guidance, children with ADHD can build confidence, improve their self-esteem, and succeed in various areas of their lives. By investing in strong communication strategies, caregivers can help children with ADHD thrive and overcome the challenges associated with their condition.

- Using positive reinforcement to encourage good behavior

Positive reinforcement is a powerful tool that can be used to encourage good behavior in individuals of all ages. This strategy involves rewarding someone for exhibiting desirable behavior, which increases the likelihood that they will continue to engage in that behavior in the future. Positive reinforcement is based on the principles of operant conditioning, a theory developed by psychologist B. F. Skinner in the mid-20th century. According to this theory, behavior that is followed by a rewarding stimulus is more likely to be repeated, while behavior that is followed by a punishing stimulus is less likely to be repeated.

One of the key advantages of using positive reinforcement to encourage good behavior is that it is a more effective and sustainable strategy than punishment. Punishment may temporarily suppress undesirable behavior, but it does not teach individuals how to engage in alternative, more appropriate behavior. In contrast, positive reinforcement focuses on rewarding and reinforcing positive behavior, which helps individuals learn and internalize the desired behavior. By consistently reinforcing good behavior with positive rewards, individuals are more likely to understand what is expected of them and to continue to exhibit that behavior in the future.

Another important benefit of using positive reinforcement is that it helps to build positive relationships and strengthen bonds between individuals. When positive reinforcement is used to encourage good behavior, individuals feel appreciated, valued, and respected. This can foster a sense of trust and mutual respect between the person providing the reinforcement and the individual receiving it. Positive reinforcement also helps to create a supportive and nurturing environment that promotes collaboration, cooperation, and a sense of belonging among group members. Ultimately, positive reinforcement can help to create a positive and harmonious social atmosphere, which can enhance overall well-being and quality of life.

Positive reinforcement can be implemented in a variety of settings, including schools, workplaces, homes, and community organizations. In educational settings, teachers can use positive reinforcement to incentivize students to engage in desired behaviors, such as completing homework assignments, participating in class discussions, and following classroom rules. By offering rewards such as praise, stickers, extra recess time, or other incentives, teachers can motivate students to stay on task and meet academic expectations. Positive reinforcement can also be used in the workplace to encourage employees to exhibit positive behaviors, such as meeting deadlines, exceeding performance goals, and collaborating effectively with colleagues. Employers can offer rewards such as bonuses, promotions, public recognition, or other incentives to reinforce good behavior and motivate employees to excel in their roles.

In addition to schools and workplaces, positive reinforcement can also be used in the home to encourage good behavior in children and family members. Parents can use positive reinforcement to reinforce desirable behaviors, such as completing chores, demonstrating good manners, or showing kindness and empathy towards others. By offering rewards such as praise, extra privileges, or special outings, parents can motivate their children to exhibit positive behaviors and develop important social and emotional skills. Positive reinforcement can also be used in community organizations to encourage positive behavior among members and promote a culture of respect, responsibility, and cooperation. By recognizing and rewarding individuals who contribute to the well-being of the community, organizations can foster a sense of belonging and unity among their members and create a positive and supportive social environment. By rewarding and reinforcing positive behaviors with incentives such as praise, rewards, or privileges, positive reinforcement can help individuals learn, internalize, and sustain desirable behaviors over time. Positive reinforcement also helps to build positive relationships and strengthen bonds between individuals, creating a supportive and nurturing environment that fosters collaboration, cooperation, and a sense of belonging. Whether in schools, workplaces, homes, or community organizations, positive reinforcement can be a powerful tool for promoting positive behavior and enhancing overall well-being and quality of life.

- Setting clear and consistent boundaries

Setting clear and consistent boundaries is essential in all aspects of life, whether it be in personal relationships, professional settings, or everyday interactions. Boundaries serve as guidelines that dictate what is acceptable and unacceptable behavior, helping to establish respect, trust, and healthy communication. Without boundaries, individuals may feel overwhelmed, disrespected, or taken advantage of, leading to conflict and misunderstandings. Therefore, it is crucial to clearly define and uphold boundaries in order to maintain positive and harmonious relationships with others.

One of the key components of setting boundaries is clearly communicating your needs, limits, and expectations to others. This involves assertively expressing your wants and desires, as well as stating what you will and will not tolerate in terms of behavior. By openly and honestly communicating your boundaries, you can help others understand your perspective and avoid misunderstandings or conflicts. Additionally, setting boundaries allows you to take ownership of your feelings and needs, empowering you to advocate for yourself and prioritize your well-being.

Consistency is another vital aspect of effective boundary-setting. It is important to maintain consistency in enforcing your boundaries and not waver in the face of pressure or manipulation. When boundaries are inconsistently enforced, it can send mixed signals to others and undermine their effectiveness. Consistency helps to establish credibility and reliability in your interactions with others, demonstrating that you are serious about upholding your boundaries and expect others to respect them as well.

In order to set clear and consistent boundaries, it is important to first identify your own values, beliefs, and priorities. By understanding what is important to you, you can establish boundaries that align with your personal values and help you maintain your integrity. Reflect on past experiences where your boundaries were violated or compromised, and consider what steps you can take to prevent similar situations in the future. It may be helpful to seek feedback from trusted friends, family members, or colleagues to gain perspective on how your boundaries are perceived by others.

When setting boundaries, it is essential to be assertive while also remaining respectful of others' perspectives. Assertiveness involves confidently expressing your needs and limits without being aggressive or disrespectful towards others. It is important to communicate your boundaries in a clear, direct, and non-confrontational manner, using "I" statements to express your feelings and expectations. By being assertive in setting boundaries, you can establish mutual respect and understanding with others, while also standing firm in upholding your own needs and values.

In addition to verbal communication, setting boundaries often involves establishing physical, emotional, and mental limits in your interactions with others. This may include setting boundaries around personal space, time commitments, emotional support, and communication preferences. For example, you may establish boundaries around when and how you are available to respond to messages or requests, or set limits on the types of topics or conversations that are acceptable in your relationships. By clearly defining these boundaries, you can create a sense of safety, predictability, and mutual understanding in your interactions with others.

It is important to remember that boundaries are not set in stone and may need to be adjusted or renegotiated over time. As circumstances change and relationships evolve, it is important to reassess your boundaries and make any necessary adjustments to ensure they continue to serve your needs and values. It is also important to be flexible and open to feedback from others, as they may have their own boundaries that need to be respected and considered in your interactions. By being open to dialogue and willing to make compromises when necessary, you can maintain healthy and respectful relationships with others while still upholding your own boundaries and priorities. By clearly defining your needs, limits, and expectations, and communicating them assertively and respectfully to others, you can create a sense of safety, predictability, and mutual understanding in your relationships. Consistency in enforcing boundaries, maintaining flexibility, and being open to feedback are also important aspects of effective boundary-setting. By prioritizing your well-being and advocating for your needs, you can establish healthy boundaries that help you navigate relationships and interactions with confidence and integrity.

Chapter 5: Managing ADHD Symptoms

- Tips for helping children cope with impulsivity

Impulsivity is a common behavior in children that can often lead to challenges in various aspects of their lives, including social interactions, academic performance, and emotional regulation. In this article, we will discuss some tips for helping children manage their impulsivity in a healthy and constructive way.

One of the first steps in helping children cope with impulsivity is to create a supportive and understanding environment. It is important for adults to recognize that impulsivity is a normal part of childhood development and that children may not have the same ability to control their impulses as adults do. By showing empathy and patience towards children who struggle with impulsivity, adults can help them feel more comfortable and supported in managing their behavior.

In addition to creating a supportive environment, adults can also teach children specific strategies for coping with impulsivity. One effective strategy is to help children learn to recognize their triggers for impulsive behavior. By identifying situations or emotions that may lead to impulsive actions, children can work on developing strategies to manage their impulses in those moments. For example, a child who tends to act impulsively when feeling frustrated may benefit from learning techniques for anger management, such as deep breathing or counting to ten before reacting.

Another important strategy for helping children cope with impulsivity is to encourage them to develop problem-solving skills. Children who struggle with impulsivity may have difficulty thinking through the consequences of their actions before acting. By teaching children to pause and consider their options before making a decision, adults can help them develop the ability to make more thoughtful and deliberate choices. Adults can also model problem-solving skills for children by talking through their own decision-making processes and sharing how they approach difficult situations.

Consistency and routine can also be helpful for children who struggle with impulsivity. By establishing clear expectations and boundaries for behavior, adults can provide children with a sense of structure and predictability that may help them feel more secure and in control. Consistent consequences for impulsive behavior can also help children understand the impact of their actions and learn to make more mindful choices in the future. It is important for adults to communicate expectations clearly and consistently, and to follow through with consequences when necessary.

In addition to these strategies, adults can also help children cope with impulsivity by providing opportunities for them to practice self-regulation skills. Activities such as mindfulness exercises, yoga, or other relaxation techniques can help children learn to calm their minds and bodies in moments of stress or impulsivity. Physical activity and play can also be beneficial for children who struggle with impulsivity, as these activities can help them release energy in a positive and healthy way. By creating a supportive environment, teaching coping strategies, encouraging problem-solving skills, maintaining consistency, and providing opportunities for self-regulation, adults can help children learn to manage their impulses in a healthy and constructive way. With support and guidance, children can develop the skills they need to navigate the challenges of impulsivity and thrive in both their academic and social lives.

- Strategies for improving focus and attention

In today's fast-paced world filled with distractions, improving focus and attention has become a crucial skill for success in both professional and academic settings. Whether you are trying to complete a complex task at work or study for an important exam, having the ability to concentrate and stay focused can significantly boost productivity and enhance your performance. However, many people struggle with maintaining their focus and attention amidst the constant barrage of emails, notifications, and other interruptions that can derail their efforts. Fortunately, there are a variety of strategies that can help individuals improve their focus and attention and achieve their goals more effectively.

One of the most effective strategies for improving focus and attention is to create a conducive environment that minimizes distractions and promotes concentration. This can involve setting up a dedicated workspace that is free from clutter and noise, and where you can focus on the task at hand without any interruptions. It's also important to turn off any unnecessary notifications on your phone or computer, as these can easily pull your attention away from what you are working on. Additionally, establishing a routine and sticking to a schedule can help train your brain to focus at specific times and improve your overall ability to maintain attention.

Another key strategy for improving focus and attention is to break down tasks into smaller, more manageable chunks. This can help prevent feelings of overwhelm and allow you to concentrate on one aspect of the task at a time, rather than trying to tackle everything at once. By setting specific, achievable goals and focusing on completing one task before moving on to the next, you can build momentum and stay engaged in the process. This approach not only helps improve your focus and attention but also ensures that you make steady progress towards your ultimate objective.

In addition to creating an optimal environment and breaking tasks into smaller segments, practicing mindfulness and meditation can also be effective in enhancing focus and attention. Mindfulness involves paying attention to the present moment without judgment, which can help improve your ability to concentrate on the task at hand and tune out distractions. Meditation, on the other hand, can help calm the mind, reduce anxiety, and improve focus through regular practice. By incorporating these techniques into your daily routine, you can train your brain to stay focused and attentive for longer periods of time.

Furthermore, staying physically active and maintaining a healthy lifestyle can also have a significant impact on your ability to focus and concentrate. Regular exercise has been shown to improve cognitive function, including attention and memory, by increasing blood flow to the brain and releasing endorphins that boost mood and energy levels. Eating a nutritious diet rich in fruits, vegetables, and whole grains can also support brain health and improve focus and attention. Additionally, getting an adequate amount of sleep is crucial for cognitive function, as lack of sleep can impair attention, memory, and decision-making abilities.

Lastly, utilizing technology and productivity tools can be beneficial in improving focus and attention. There are a variety of apps and tools available that can help you stay organized, set goals, and track progress on tasks. For example, time management apps can help you prioritize tasks and allocate your time effectively, while focus apps can block distractions and keep you on track. Additionally, using techniques such as the Pomodoro method, which involves working in short bursts with breaks in between, can help improve focus and prevent burnout. By creating a conducive environment, breaking tasks into manageable chunks, practicing mindfulness and meditation, staying physically active, maintaining a healthy lifestyle, and utilizing technology and productivity tools, individuals can significantly enhance their ability to concentrate and achieve their goals. By incorporating these strategies into your daily routine, you can improve your focus and attention, boost productivity, and ultimately succeed in both your professional and academic pursuits.

- How to manage hyperactivity in children with ADHD

Attention Deficit Hyperactivity Disorder (ADHD) is a neurodevelopmental disorder characterized by a pattern of inattentiveness, impulsivity, and hyperactivity that can significantly impact a child's ability to function in everyday life. Children with ADHD may struggle with tasks that require sustained attention, organization, and impulse control, making it challenging for them to excel academically and socially. One of the core symptoms of ADHD is hyperactivity, which involves excessive motor activity, fidgeting, and restlessness. Managing hyperactivity in children with ADHD requires a comprehensive approach that addresses both the underlying neurobiological factors contributing to the hyperactivity and the environmental factors that can exacerbate symptoms.

There are several evidence-based strategies that parents and educators can implement to help manage hyperactivity in children with ADHD. One of the first steps in managing hyperactivity is to establish a structured routine for the child that includes predictable activities and consistent daily schedules. Children with ADHD often benefit from clear expectations and routines that provide a sense of stability and predictability. This can help reduce anxiety and impulsivity, which are common triggers for hyperactivity. Additionally, incorporating regular breaks and physical activity into the child's day can help channel excess energy and reduce restlessness. Encouraging the child to engage in activities that involve movement, such as sports, dance, or yoga, can also be beneficial in managing hyperactivity.

In addition to establishing a structured routine, it is important to create a supportive and stimulating environment for children with ADHD. This may involve minimizing distractions in the child's surroundings, such as loud noises, clutter, or bright lights, that can heighten hyperactivity. Creating a calm and organized workspace for the child can help improve focus and concentration, making it easier for them to manage their hyperactivity. Providing consistent praise and positive reinforcement for desired behaviors can also help motivate the child to self-regulate and control their impulses. Setting clear boundaries and consequences for inappropriate behavior can help teach the child about cause and effect and promote self-control.

Another important aspect of managing hyperactivity in children with ADHD is implementing behavioral strategies that target specific hyperactive behaviors. One effective strategy is the use of praise and rewards to reinforce positive behaviors and encourage self-regulation. By acknowledging and rewarding the child's efforts to control their hyperactivity, parents and educators can help build their self-esteem and motivation to improve. It is important to be consistent in providing praise and rewards for desired behaviors, as this can help reinforce positive habits and reduce the frequency of hyperactive behaviors.

In addition to praise and rewards, behavioral strategies such as token economies and response cost systems can be effective in managing hyperactivity in children with ADHD. Token economies involve rewarding the child with tokens or points for demonstrating desired behaviors, which can then be exchanged for privileges or rewards. This system can help motivate the child to control their hyperactivity and focus on positive behaviors. Response cost systems involve imposing consequences, such as loss of privileges or tokens, for engaging in hyperactive behaviors. By implementing these strategies consistently, parents and educators can help the child learn to self-regulate their impulses and manage their hyperactivity.

It is important to remember that every child with ADHD is unique and may respond differently to various management strategies. Therefore, it is important to work closely with a healthcare provider or mental health professional to develop a personalized plan for managing hyperactivity in children with ADHD. In some cases, medication may be prescribed to help manage symptoms of hyperactivity and improve the child's ability to focus and stay calm. However, medication should always be used in combination with behavioral strategies and environmental modifications to ensure the most effective treatment approach. By implementing structured routines, creating a supportive environment, and utilizing behavioral strategies, parents and educators can help children with ADHD learn to self-regulate their impulses and manage their hyperactivity effectively. It is important to remember that managing hyperactivity in children with ADHD is a collaborative effort that requires patience, consistency, and understanding. With the right support and guidance, children with ADHD can learn to thrive and reach their full potential.

Chapter 6: Building Self-esteem and Resilience

- Importance of building self-esteem in children with ADHD

Self-esteem plays a crucial role in the development and well-being of children, especially those with Attention-Deficit/Hyperactivity Disorder (ADHD). ADHD is a neurodevelopmental disorder characterized by symptoms of inattention, impulsivity, and hyperactivity. Children with ADHD often face challenges in academic performance, social interactions, and emotional regulation. Building self-esteem in children with ADHD is essential to help them overcome these challenges and reach their full potential.

One of the primary reasons why building self-esteem is crucial for children with ADHD is because it helps them develop a positive self-image. Children with ADHD may struggle with feelings of inadequacy, frustration, and low self-worth due to their difficulties in focusing, organizing tasks, and controlling impulses. By building self-esteem, children with ADHD can develop a stronger sense of self-confidence and self-worth, which can help them navigate the challenges of their disorder more effectively.

Moreover, building self-esteem in children with ADHD can also improve their academic performance. Children with ADHD may struggle with staying focused in class, completing assignments on time, and retaining information due to their difficulties in attention and impulse control. By building their self-esteem, children with ADHD can develop a growth mindset and resilience that enables them to persevere through academic challenges and setbacks.

In addition to academic performance, building self-esteem in children with ADHD can also enhance their social skills and relationships. Children with ADHD may exhibit impulsive behaviors, difficulty following social cues, and challenges in forming and maintaining friendships. Low self-esteem can exacerbate these difficulties, leading to feelings of isolation, rejection, and loneliness. By building their self-esteem, children with ADHD can develop more positive social interactions, effective communication skills, and healthy relationships with peers and adults.

Furthermore, building self-esteem in children with ADHD can also improve their emotional regulation and mental health. Children with ADHD may experience intense emotions, mood swings, and difficulty managing their feelings due to their neurological differences. Low self-esteem can contribute to emotional dysregulation, anxiety, and depression in children with ADHD. By building their self-esteem, children with ADHD can develop coping mechanisms, emotional intelligence, and self-awareness that help them manage their emotions more effectively and promote their mental well-being. It helps them develop a positive self-image, improve their academic performance, enhance their social skills and relationships, and promote their emotional regulation and mental health. Parents, educators, and mental health professionals can support children with ADHD in building their self-esteem through positive reinforcement, encouragement, praise, and opportunities for success. By fostering self-esteem in children with ADHD, we can empower them to overcome their challenges, embrace their strengths, and thrive in all aspects of their lives.

- Strategies for helping children develop resilience

Resilience is a crucial skill for children to develop, as it equips them with the ability to navigate challenges and setbacks effectively. By building resilience, children are better equipped to handle stress, adversity, and uncertainty in their lives. There are several strategies that parents, teachers, and caregivers can employ to help children develop resilience.

One important strategy for fostering resilience in children is to build strong relationships with them. Positive relationships with adults who care for and support them provide children with a sense of security and stability. When children feel safe and loved, they are more likely to develop the confidence and self-esteem needed to overcome challenges. Parents and caregivers can nurture these relationships by spending quality time with children, listening to their thoughts and feelings, and offering encouragement and guidance.

Another key strategy for developing resilience in children is to teach them problem-solving skills. Children who are able to think critically and creatively about problems are better equipped to find solutions and adapt to difficult situations. Parents and teachers can help children develop these skills by encouraging them to brainstorm solutions, make decisions independently, and learn from their mistakes. By fostering a growth mindset in children, adults can instill in them the belief that they can improve and overcome obstacles through effort and persistence.

In addition to building strong relationships and problem-solving skills, it is important to teach children how to regulate their emotions. Emotion regulation is a critical component of resilience, as it helps children manage stress and negative emotions effectively. Parents and caregivers can help children develop this skill by modeling healthy emotional expression, teaching them relaxation techniques such as deep breathing or mindfulness, and providing them with opportunities to practice coping strategies when faced with challenging situations.

Furthermore, it is essential for adults to foster a sense of autonomy and independence in children. When children are given opportunities to make choices and take on responsibilities, they develop a sense of agency and control over their lives. This sense of autonomy can help children feel empowered and capable of facing challenges with confidence. Parents and teachers can support children in developing autonomy by providing them with age-appropriate tasks and responsibilities, encouraging them to make decisions independently, and praising their efforts and accomplishments.

It is important to help children develop a sense of perspective and optimism. By teaching children to reframe negative situations in a positive light, adults can help them build resilience and maintain a positive outlook on life. Parents and caregivers can help children develop this skill by emphasizing the importance of gratitude, encouraging them to focus on their strengths and accomplishments, and helping them see challenges as opportunities for growth and learning. By building strong relationships, teaching problem-solving skills, fostering emotional regulation, promoting autonomy, and encouraging a positive perspective, adults can help children develop the resilience needed to thrive in the face of adversity. With the right support and guidance, children can learn to navigate life's ups and downs with courage, strength, and perseverance.

- Encouraging independence and self-confidence

Encouraging independence and self-confidence in individuals is vital for their overall growth and development. By instilling a sense of autonomy and self-reliance, individuals are better equipped to navigate life's challenges and seize opportunities for personal and professional success. Independence allows individuals to make their own decisions, take responsibility for their actions, and learn from both their successes and failures. Self-confidence, on the other hand, empowers individuals to believe in their abilities and trust their judgment, leading to greater resilience and perseverance in the face of obstacles.

One way to encourage independence and self-confidence is to provide individuals with opportunities to make choices and take ownership of their decisions. This can be done in various settings, such as at home, in school, or in the workplace. For example, parents can empower their children to make decisions about their education, extracurricular activities, and social interactions. Similarly, teachers can involve students in setting learning goals, choosing projects, and evaluating their progress. In the workplace, managers can delegate tasks, provide autonomy in decision-making, and offer opportunities for self-directed learning and professional development. By giving individuals the freedom to make choices and take responsibility for their actions, they can develop a sense of agency and self-efficacy.

Another way to promote independence and self-confidence is to provide support and encouragement along the way. While independence involves taking initiative and being self-reliant, it does not mean going it alone. Individuals benefit from having mentors, coaches, and role models who can guide, advise, and inspire them. Supportive relationships can boost self-confidence, provide emotional validation, and offer constructive feedback. By fostering a sense of belonging and connectedness, individuals feel empowered to take risks, explore new opportunities, and overcome challenges. Encouraging independence does not mean abandoning individuals to figure things out on their own; rather, it means equipping them with the tools, resources, and support they need to succeed.

Furthermore, promoting independence and self-confidence requires creating environments that foster growth, learning, and experimentation. This can be achieved by encouraging individuals to set ambitious goals, take on new challenges, and embrace change. Creating a culture of continuous learning and improvement helps individuals develop resilience, adaptability, and a growth mindset. Failure is viewed not as a setback but as a valuable learning opportunity. By celebrating effort, progress, and perseverance, individuals feel motivated to push themselves beyond their comfort zones and reach their full potential. This emphasis on growth and development cultivates a sense of self-efficacy and resilience that is essential for building confidence and independence. By empowering individuals to make choices, take ownership of their decisions, and learn from their experiences, they can develop a sense of agency and self-efficacy. Providing support, guidance, and encouragement along the way helps individuals feel confident, capable, and motivated to pursue their goals. Creating environments that foster growth, learning, and experimentation cultivates resilience, adaptability, and a growth mindset that are crucial for success. Ultimately, by promoting independence and self-confidence, individuals can lead fulfilling and meaningful lives, both personally and professionally.

Chapter 7: Nurturing Emotional Wellbeing

- Understanding the emotional challenges faced by children with ADHD

Attention-deficit/hyperactivity disorder (ADHD) is a neurodevelopmental disorder that affects millions of children worldwide. Children with ADHD often struggle with impulsivity, inattention, and hyperactivity, which can impact their ability to succeed in school, maintain relationships, and regulate their emotions. One of the most challenging aspects of ADHD is the emotional dysregulation that many children experience. Emotional dysregulation refers to difficulty in controlling or expressing emotions in a socially appropriate manner. This can manifest in explosive outbursts, mood swings, and difficulty in handling stress and frustration.

Children with ADHD may have difficulty in recognizing and regulating their emotions, which can lead to challenges in social interactions and relationships. They may struggle to understand and interpret the emotions of others, leading to misunderstandings and conflicts. Additionally, the impulsivity and hyperactivity characteristic of ADHD can exacerbate emotional dysregulation, as children may act out without considering the consequences of their actions. These emotional challenges can significantly impact a child's self-esteem and sense of self-worth, as they may feel misunderstood or unable to control their emotions.

It is important for parents, educators, and mental health professionals to understand the emotional challenges faced by children with ADHD in order to provide appropriate support and intervention. One common misconception is that children with ADHD are simply misbehaving or being deliberately difficult. In reality, their emotional dysregulation is a symptom of their neurodevelopmental disorder and requires a different approach to management. By recognizing and acknowledging the emotional challenges faced by these children, we can create a more empathetic and supportive environment that fosters their emotional growth and well-being.

There are several strategies that can help children with ADHD manage their emotional challenges more effectively. First and foremost, it is essential to provide a structured and predictable environment that minimizes stress and promotes emotional regulation. This may include establishing clear routines, setting clear expectations, and providing regular breaks to help children regulate their emotions. In addition, teaching children relaxation techniques, such as deep breathing or mindfulness exercises, can help them cope with stress and anxiety. Encouraging children to express their feelings and emotions in a healthy way, such as through journaling or talking to a trusted adult, can also be beneficial in developing their emotional awareness and coping skills.

Furthermore, it is important for parents and educators to set realistic expectations for children with ADHD and to provide consistent praise and positive reinforcement for their efforts. Building a strong support network of family members, teachers, and mental health professionals can also be invaluable in helping children with ADHD navigate their emotional challenges. By working together and advocating for the needs of these children, we can create a more inclusive and understanding community that supports their emotional well-being and overall success. By recognizing and addressing their emotional dysregulation, we can help children with ADHD develop the coping skills and emotional awareness necessary to navigate the complexities of their disorder. Through a combination of structured environments, relaxation techniques, emotional expression, and positive reinforcement, we can empower these children to overcome their emotional challenges and reach their full potential. By fostering a culture of empathy and support, we can create a brighter future for children with ADHD and ensure that they receive the understanding and care they deserve.

- Tips for helping children manage their emotions

Managing emotions can be a challenging task for anyone, but for children, it can be even more difficult due to their limited understanding of their emotions and how to handle them effectively. As adults, it is our responsibility to help children navigate their emotions in a healthy way to ensure their emotional well-being. In this article, we will discuss some tips for helping children manage their emotions.

First and foremost, it is essential to teach children about emotions and help them understand that it is normal to experience a wide range of emotions. By educating children about emotions, they can learn to recognize and label their feelings, which is the first step in managing them effectively. Encourage children to express their emotions in a safe and healthy way, whether it be through talking, drawing, or using other forms of creative expression.

Another important tip for helping children manage their emotions is to teach them effective coping strategies. Encourage children to take deep breaths, count to ten, or engage in physical activities such as running or jumping to help regulate their emotions. Encourage children to problem-solve and find solutions to the situations that are causing them distress. By teaching children these coping strategies, they can learn to handle their emotions in a constructive way.

Furthermore, it is crucial to set a positive example for children when it comes to managing emotions. Children learn by watching the adults in their lives, so it is essential to model healthy emotional regulation. Be mindful of how you express your own emotions around children and show them how to handle difficult situations calmly and rationally. By setting a positive example, children can learn how to manage their emotions effectively.

Additionally, it is important to create a safe and supportive environment for children to express their emotions. Encourage open communication and create a safe space where children feel comfortable sharing their feelings without judgment. Validate their emotions and let them know that it is okay to feel what they are feeling. By creating a safe and supportive environment, children will be more likely to open up about their emotions and seek help when needed. By teaching children about emotions, providing them with coping strategies, setting a positive example, and creating a safe and supportive environment, we can help children develop the skills they need to navigate their emotions effectively. By working together as adults to support children in managing their emotions, we can help them grow into emotionally healthy and resilient individuals.

- Importance of seeking professional help when needed

Seeking professional help when needed is crucial for addressing various mental health concerns and improving overall well-being. While many individuals may feel hesitant or ashamed to reach out for assistance, it is important to understand that seeking help is a sign of strength and resilience. Mental health professionals are trained to provide support, guidance, and interventions to help individuals navigate their challenges and develop coping mechanisms. By seeking professional help, individuals can gain a better understanding of their thoughts, emotions, and behaviors, leading to improved self-awareness and overall mental health.

One of the key reasons why seeking professional help is important is that mental health issues can impact all aspects of an individual's life, including relationships, work, and physical health. Without proper support and intervention, these issues can worsen over time and have a detrimental impact on the individual's overall well-being. Mental health professionals can help individuals identify the root causes of their problems, develop a treatment plan tailored to their needs, and provide ongoing support to help them achieve their goals.

In addition to addressing mental health concerns, seeking professional help can also help individuals build resilience and develop effective coping skills. Mental health professionals can teach individuals techniques for managing stress, regulating emotions, and improving communication skills, all of which are essential for maintaining good mental health. By learning how to cope with challenges in a healthy and constructive manner, individuals can improve their ability to navigate difficult situations and build a strong foundation for long-term mental wellness.

Furthermore, seeking professional help can help individuals overcome feelings of isolation and loneliness that often accompany mental health issues. Many individuals may feel like they are alone in their struggles and that no one understands what they are going through. Mental health professionals provide a safe and non-judgmental space for individuals to express their thoughts and feelings, receive validation and support, and connect with others who are facing similar challenges. This sense of connection and community can be incredibly empowering and can help individuals feel less alone in their journey towards mental wellness.

It is also important to recognize that mental health issues are not a sign of weakness or failure. Just as individuals seek medical help for physical ailments, it is important to seek professional help for mental health concerns. Mental health is just as important as physical health and should be given the same level of attention and care. By reaching out for support, individuals can take proactive steps towards improving their mental health and overall quality of life. Mental health professionals are trained to provide the support, guidance, and interventions necessary for individuals to navigate their challenges, develop coping skills, and achieve their goals. It is important for individuals to recognize that seeking help is a sign of strength and resilience, and that mental health is just as important as physical health. By reaching out for support, individuals can take proactive steps towards improving their mental health and living a fulfilling and meaningful life.

Chapter 8: Enhancing Social Skills

- Importance of developing social skills in children with ADHD

Children diagnosed with ADHD often face challenges in social situations due to their hyperactivity, impulsivity, and difficulty focusing on social cues. This can lead to difficulties in forming and maintaining relationships with peers, as well as in understanding social norms and appropriate behavior. As such, it is crucial for parents, teachers, and mental health professionals to focus on developing social skills in children with ADHD in order to help them navigate social interactions more effectively and build meaningful connections with others.

One of the key reasons why developing social skills in children with ADHD is important is because it can help improve their overall well-being and quality of life. Research has shown that children with ADHD who have strong social skills are more likely to have positive self-esteem, perform better academically, and experience fewer behavioral problems. By improving their ability to communicate effectively, resolve conflicts, and show empathy towards others, children with ADHD can build stronger relationships and feel more confident in their social interactions.

Furthermore, developing social skills in children with ADHD can also help them succeed in their academic and professional endeavors. Social skills play a crucial role in the workplace, as individuals are required to collaborate with others, communicate effectively, and navigate social dynamics. By teaching children with ADHD how to interact with peers, teachers, and other authority figures in a positive and respectful manner, we can help prepare them for success in school and future career opportunities.

In addition to improving their overall well-being and academic success, developing social skills in children with ADHD can also help reduce feelings of isolation and loneliness. Children with ADHD often struggle to make friends and feel socially isolated, which can have a negative impact on their mental health and emotional well-being. By teaching them how to engage in social interactions, read social cues, and respond appropriately to social situations, we can help children with ADHD build a supportive network of friends and peers who understand and accept them for who they are.

It is important to note that developing social skills in children with ADHD is not a one-size-fits-all approach. Each child is unique and may require individualized strategies and interventions to help them improve their social skills. However, there are several evidence-based techniques that have been shown to be effective in helping children with ADHD develop their social skills.

One such technique is social skills training, which involves teaching children with ADHD specific social skills and strategies through role-playing, modeling, and feedback. By practicing these skills in a safe and supportive environment, children with ADHD can gain confidence and competence in their social interactions. Another effective approach is cognitive-behavioral therapy, which helps children with ADHD identify and challenge negative thought patterns and behaviors that may be hindering their social skills development.

In addition to these therapeutic interventions, parents and teachers can also play a crucial role in helping children with ADHD develop their social skills. By providing consistent guidance, support, and encouragement, parents and teachers can help children with ADHD learn how to navigate social situations, communicate effectively, and build positive relationships with others. It is important for parents and teachers to be patient and understanding, as developing social skills takes time and practice. By teaching children with ADHD how to communicate effectively, resolve conflicts, and interact with others in a positive and respectful manner, we can help them build strong relationships and navigate social situations more effectively. With the right support and guidance from parents, teachers, and mental health professionals, children with ADHD can develop the social skills they need to thrive at school, at work, and in their personal lives.

- Strategies for improving social interactions

Social interactions play a significant role in our daily lives, influencing our relationships, personal and professional success, and overall well-being. However, for some individuals, navigating social interactions can be challenging and sometimes even daunting. Fortunately, there are several strategies that can help improve social interactions and enhance communication skills.

One key strategy for improving social interactions is to practice active listening. Active listening involves fully engaging with the speaker, paying attention to both their words and nonverbal cues, and providing feedback that demonstrates understanding. By actively listening, you show respect and empathy towards the other person, which can help build rapport and strengthen relationships. Additionally, active listening can help avoid misunderstandings and miscommunications, fostering more effective and meaningful interactions.

Another effective strategy for improving social interactions is to work on developing strong communication skills. This includes not only verbal communication but also nonverbal communication such as body language, facial expressions, and tone of voice. By improving your communication skills, you can convey your thoughts and emotions more clearly and effectively, leading to better understanding and connection with others. Additionally, being mindful of your nonverbal cues can help you better interpret the emotions and intentions of others, facilitating more empathetic and authentic interactions.

In addition to active listening and communication skills, cultivating emotional intelligence can also play a significant role in improving social interactions. Emotional intelligence involves being aware of and managing your emotions, as well as recognizing and understanding the emotions of others. By developing emotional intelligence, you can better regulate your own emotions in social situations, respond more effectively to the emotions of others, and build stronger relationships based on empathy and understanding. This can lead to more harmonious and fulfilling social interactions, both in personal and professional settings.

Furthermore, practicing assertiveness can be a valuable strategy for improving social interactions. Being assertive involves expressing your thoughts, feelings, and needs in a clear and respectful manner, while also listening to and respecting the perspectives of others. By asserting yourself in a confident and assertive manner, you can establish boundaries, communicate effectively, and advocate for yourself in social interactions. This can lead to more authentic and balanced relationships, where both parties feel heard, respected, and valued.

Lastly, seeking out opportunities for social engagement and practicing social skills in real-world settings can also be beneficial for improving social interactions. This may involve joining social clubs or groups, attending networking events, or participating in activities that allow you to meet new people and practice your social skills in a supportive and non-judgmental environment. By stepping out of your comfort zone and engaging with others, you can enhance your social skills, build confidence, and expand your social network, ultimately leading to more fulfilling and enriching social interactions. By practicing active listening, developing strong communication skills, cultivating emotional intelligence, being assertive, and seeking out social engagement opportunities, you can enhance your social interactions, build stronger relationships, and improve your overall well-being. Remember that improving social interactions is a continuous process that requires practice, patience, and a willingness to learn and grow. With dedication and effort, you can enhance your social skills and enjoy more meaningful and rewarding interactions with others.

- Encouraging healthy peer relationships

Peer relationships are an integral aspect of human development, particularly during childhood and adolescence. Healthy peer relationships can have a positive impact on a person's mental health, self-esteem, and ability to navigate complex social situations. However, fostering these positive relationships can sometimes be challenging, especially in today's fast-paced and digitally driven world.

One key factor in promoting healthy peer relationships is creating environments that encourage open communication and empathy. When individuals feel comfortable expressing their thoughts and emotions to their peers, it fosters a sense of trust and mutual respect. By teaching children and adolescents how to effectively communicate and listen to others, we can help them develop the skills needed to build strong and lasting relationships. Encouraging empathy is also crucial, as it allows individuals to put themselves in others' shoes and understand their perspectives and feelings. Empathy can help reduce conflicts and misunderstandings, leading to healthier and more harmonious peer interactions.

Another important aspect of promoting healthy peer relationships is teaching individuals how to set boundaries and respect the boundaries of others. Boundaries are essential for maintaining healthy relationships and ensuring that all individuals feel safe and respected. By establishing clear boundaries and communicating them effectively, individuals can avoid potentially harmful situations and conflicts. Respecting the boundaries of others is equally important, as it demonstrates empathy and consideration for their feelings and needs. By encouraging individuals to assert their boundaries and respect those of others, we can create a culture of mutual respect and understanding within peer groups.

In addition to communication and boundaries, promoting positive peer relationships also involves fostering a sense of inclusivity and diversity within groups. Encouraging individuals to embrace diversity and accept others for who they are can help create a more inclusive and welcoming environment for everyone. By celebrating differences and promoting acceptance, we can help individuals feel valued and appreciated for their unique qualities and experiences. This sense of inclusivity can lead to stronger bonds and friendships among peers, as it creates a sense of belonging and unity within the group.

Furthermore, promoting healthy peer relationships involves addressing issues such as bullying, cliques, and peer pressure. These negative dynamics can have a detrimental impact on individuals' mental health and self-esteem, leading to feelings of isolation, exclusion, and insecurity. By educating individuals about the harmful effects of bullying and peer pressure, we can empower them to stand up against these negative behaviors and support those who are being targeted. Encouraging individuals to be inclusive and welcoming to others can help reduce cliques and promote a more positive and supportive peer culture. By fostering these key aspects, we can help individuals develop the skills and attitudes needed to build strong and fulfilling relationships with their peers. By prioritizing the importance of healthy peer relationships, we can contribute to creating a more positive and supportive social environment for all individuals.

Chapter 9: Supporting Academic Success

- Tips for helping children with ADHD succeed in school

Attention Deficit Hyperactivity Disorder (ADHD) is a neurodevelopmental disorder that affects many children around the world. Children with ADHD often struggle with inattention, hyperactivity, and impulsivity, which can make it challenging for them to succeed in school. However, with the right support and strategies in place, children with ADHD can thrive academically. In this article, we will discuss tips for helping children with ADHD succeed in school.

One of the first and most important steps in helping children with ADHD succeed in school is to create a structured and predictable environment. Children with ADHD thrive on routine and structure, so it is important to establish clear routines and schedules for them to follow. This can help minimize distractions and provide a sense of stability for the child. Creating a visual schedule or checklist can also be helpful in keeping the child organized and on track. By providing structure and predictability, children with ADHD can better focus on their schoolwork and succeed academically.

Another important tip for helping children with ADHD succeed in school is to break tasks down into smaller, manageable steps. Children with ADHD can become easily overwhelmed by tasks that seem too big or complex. By breaking tasks down into smaller steps, it can help the child stay organized and focused. For example, if a child has a large project to complete, break it down into smaller tasks such as researching, writing, and editing. This can help the child feel more in control and motivated to complete the task.

In addition to breaking tasks down into smaller steps, it is also important to provide plenty of breaks and opportunities for movement for children with ADHD. Children with ADHD often have a lot of energy and may struggle to sit still for long periods of time. Allowing the child to take breaks and move around can help them release excess energy and refocus when they return to their schoolwork. Encouraging physical activities such as stretching, walking, or even jumping jacks can help the child stay alert and engaged in their schoolwork.

Furthermore, it is important to provide positive reinforcement and praise for children with ADHD. Children with ADHD can often struggle with low self-esteem and motivation, so providing praise and encouragement can help boost their confidence and motivation. Recognize and celebrate the child's small accomplishments and improvements, no matter how minor they may seem. Positive reinforcement can help the child feel more confident in their abilities and encourage them to continue working hard in school.

Additionally, it is important to work closely with teachers and school staff to support children with ADHD in the classroom. Teachers play a crucial role in helping children with ADHD succeed in school, so it is important to communicate regularly with them about the child's needs and progress. Collaborate with teachers to create a personalized education plan for the child with accommodations and supports that can help them succeed. This may include extra time on assignments, preferential seating, or breaks during class. By working together with teachers, parents can help ensure that the child's educational needs are being met and that they have the support they need to succeed in school.

Another helpful tip for supporting children with ADHD in school is to teach them effective study and organizational skills. Children with ADHD may struggle with time management, organization, and planning, so it is important to teach them strategies for staying organized and on top of their schoolwork. This can include using a planner or calendar to track assignments and due dates, breaking tasks down into manageable chunks, and setting aside specific time for homework and studying each day. By teaching children with ADHD how to effectively manage their time and stay organized, it can help them become more independent and successful in school. By creating a structured and predictable environment, breaking tasks down into manageable steps, providing breaks and opportunities for movement, offering positive reinforcement and praise, working closely with teachers, and teaching effective study and organizational skills, children with ADHD can thrive academically. With patience, understanding, and support from parents, teachers, and school staff, children with ADHD can reach their full potential and succeed in school.

- Strategies for managing homework and study habits

Homework and study habits are essential components of academic success. By developing effective strategies for managing these tasks, students can improve their learning outcomes and ultimately achieve their academic goals. In this article, we will discuss some practical tips and techniques for managing homework and study habits.

One of the first steps in managing homework and study habits is to create a study schedule. This schedule should include dedicated time for completing homework assignments, as well as time for studying and reviewing material for upcoming tests or exams. By having a structured study schedule, students can ensure that they are allocating enough time to each task and are not procrastinating or leaving things until the last minute. Additionally, having a study schedule can help students stay organized and on track with their academic responsibilities.

Another important aspect of managing homework and study habits is to create a conducive study environment. This includes finding a quiet and comfortable space to work, free from distractions such as noise, electronics, or other people. By having a dedicated study space, students can focus their attention on their work and maximize their productivity. It is also helpful to have all necessary materials and supplies on hand, such as textbooks, notebooks, pens, and calculators, to avoid interruptions or distractions while studying.

Effective time management is also key to managing homework and study habits. By prioritizing tasks and setting specific goals for each study session, students can make the most of their time and ensure that they are making progress towards their academic objectives. One useful technique for improving time management is the Pomodoro technique, which involves working for a set period of time (typically 25 minutes) followed by a short break. This can help students stay focused and motivated while studying, and can prevent burnout or fatigue from long periods of uninterrupted study.

In addition to time management, it is important for students to develop effective study strategies. This may include techniques such as active reading, summarizing material, creating flashcards, or practicing example problems. By using different study strategies, students can engage with the material in a variety of ways and improve their understanding and retention of the material. It is also beneficial to review and revise material regularly, rather than cramming all the information at once, as this can help reinforce learning and improve long-term retention.

Another important aspect of managing homework and study habits is to seek help and support when needed. This may involve reaching out to teachers or professors for clarification on assignments or concepts, forming study groups with peers to collaborate and discuss material, or seeking tutoring or academic support services. By asking for help when needed, students can gain a deeper understanding of the material and improve their academic performance. It is also important for students to take care of their physical and mental well-being, as this can have a significant impact on their ability to focus and concentrate while studying. This may involve getting enough sleep, eating healthily, exercising regularly, and taking breaks when needed to rest and recharge. By creating a study schedule, establishing a conducive study environment, managing time effectively, developing study strategies, seeking help and support when needed, and taking care of physical and mental well-being, students can improve their learning outcomes and achieve their academic goals. By implementing these strategies and techniques, students can maximize their potential and succeed in their academic endeavors.

- Importance of working with teachers and school staff

Working collaboratively with teachers and school staff is integral to the success of a school community. The importance of fostering positive relationships and teamwork among educators cannot be overstated. It is essential for achieving the common goal of providing a high-quality education for students. When teachers and staff work together effectively, they can create a supportive and nurturing environment that enhances student learning and well-being.

One of the key reasons why it is important to work closely with teachers and school staff is the impact it has on student outcomes. Research has consistently shown that strong collaboration among educators leads to improved academic achievement for students. When teachers and staff work together cohesively, they are better able to address the diverse needs of students and provide targeted support where it is needed most. This collaborative approach can also result in more effective classroom management and a more engaging and dynamic learning experience for students.

In addition to improving student outcomes, working with teachers and school staff can also enhance professional development opportunities for educators. Collaboration allows educators to share best practices, strategies, and resources with one another, leading to a continuous cycle of learning and growth. By working together, teachers and staff can collaborate on lesson planning, curriculum development, and assessment strategies, ultimately strengthening their instructional practices and improving their ability to meet the needs of all students.

Furthermore, working collaboratively with teachers and school staff can help create a positive and inclusive school culture. When educators work together as a team, they model cooperation and respect for one another, which can have a ripple effect throughout the entire school community. Collaboration fosters a sense of unity and solidarity among educators, leading to increased morale, job satisfaction, and ultimately, a more supportive and nurturing environment for students.

Another important aspect of working with teachers and school staff is the opportunity it provides for creating a sense of community within the school. By collaborating with one another, educators can build strong relationships and networks that extend beyond the classroom. This sense of community can help foster a positive school culture, where teachers and staff feel supported, valued, and respected. This, in turn, can lead to increased job satisfaction, retention rates, and overall school morale. Collaboration among educators is essential for improving student outcomes, enhancing professional development opportunities, creating a positive school culture, and fostering a sense of community within the school. By working together as a cohesive team, educators can provide a high-quality education for all students and create a supportive and nurturing environment where students can thrive. It is crucial for school leaders to prioritize collaboration and teamwork among educators, as it is the foundation for a successful and effective school community.

Chapter 10: Collaborating with Healthcare Professionals

- Importance of working with healthcare professionals in managing ADHD

Attention-deficit/hyperactivity disorder (ADHD) is a common neurodevelopmental disorder that affects both children and adults. It is characterized by symptoms of inattention, impulsivity, and hyperactivity, which can have a significant impact on daily functioning and quality of life. Managing ADHD requires a comprehensive and multidisciplinary approach, involving not only the individual with ADHD but also their parents, teachers, and healthcare professionals.

One of the most important aspects of managing ADHD is working closely with healthcare professionals who specialize in the diagnosis and treatment of the disorder. These professionals may include psychiatrists, psychologists, pediatricians, and neurologists, among others. They play a crucial role in assessing the individual's symptoms, making an accurate diagnosis, and developing a personalized treatment plan.

Healthcare professionals can provide valuable insights into the underlying causes of ADHD and offer evidence-based treatments that have been proven effective in managing the disorder. They can prescribe medication, such as stimulant medications or non-stimulant alternatives, which can help alleviate symptoms of inattention and hyperactivity. Additionally, they can recommend behavioral therapies, such as cognitive-behavioral therapy or parent training, which can help individuals with ADHD learn coping strategies and improve their executive functioning skills.

Working with healthcare professionals also ensures that individuals with ADHD receive ongoing monitoring and support throughout the treatment process. Healthcare professionals can regularly evaluate the individual's progress, adjust their treatment plan as needed, and address any concerns or challenges that may arise. This level of personalized care and attention is essential for optimizing treatment outcomes and improving the individual's overall well-being.

Furthermore, healthcare professionals can help individuals with ADHD navigate the complexities of the healthcare system and access the resources and support they need. They can provide information about community resources, support groups, and educational programs that can be beneficial for individuals with ADHD and their families. By working collaboratively with healthcare professionals, individuals with ADHD can build a strong support network and receive comprehensive care that addresses their unique needs and challenges. These professionals have the expertise, knowledge, and skills to assess, diagnose, and treat the disorder, and they can provide valuable support and guidance throughout the treatment process. By collaborating with healthcare professionals, individuals with ADHD can receive the personalized care and attention they need to improve their symptoms, enhance their functioning, and lead a more fulfilling and productive life.

- Understanding the different treatment options available

When it comes to seeking treatment for a variety of health conditions, it's important to understand the different options available in order to make an informed decision. There are a wide range of treatment options available, each with their own benefits and drawbacks. By understanding the different treatment options, individuals can work with their healthcare provider to determine the best course of action for their specific needs.

One of the most common treatment options available is medication. Medications can be prescribed to help manage symptoms, control disease progression, or even cure certain conditions. It's important to follow your healthcare provider's recommendations when taking medications, as they can have potential side effects and interactions with other medications. It's also important to communicate openly with your healthcare provider about any concerns or issues you may have with your medication regimen.

Another treatment option that is often used in conjunction with medication is therapy. Therapy can come in many forms, including talk therapy, cognitive behavioral therapy, or group therapy. Therapy can be a valuable tool in helping individuals cope with the emotional and psychological aspects of their condition. It can also help individuals develop coping strategies and improve their overall quality of life. If you are considering therapy as a treatment option, it's important to find a qualified and experienced therapist who specializes in your specific condition.

In addition to medication and therapy, there are a number of alternative treatment options that individuals may consider. These can include acupuncture, massage therapy, chiropractic care, or herbal remedies. While these alternative treatments may not be supported by as much scientific evidence as traditional treatments, some individuals find them to be helpful in managing their symptoms and improving their quality of life. It's important to discuss any alternative treatments with your healthcare provider to ensure they are safe and effective for your specific condition.

Surgery is another treatment option that may be recommended for certain health conditions. Surgery can be used to remove tumors, repair damaged tissues, or correct structural abnormalities. It's important to understand the risks and benefits of surgery before making a decision, as surgery can be a major undertaking with potential complications. Your healthcare provider can help you weigh the risks and benefits of surgery and determine if it is the right treatment option for you.

Lastly, lifestyle modifications can also be an important part of a treatment plan. This can include changes to diet, exercise, sleep habits, and stress management techniques. Lifestyle modifications can help improve overall health and well-being, and may even reduce the need for medication or other treatments. It's important to work with your healthcare provider to develop a personalized plan for lifestyle modifications that are tailored to your specific needs and goals. By understanding the different treatment options and working closely with your healthcare provider, you can develop a personalized treatment plan that meets your specific needs and goals. Whether you are considering medication, therapy, surgery, alternative treatments, or lifestyle modifications, it's important to make informed decisions and actively participate in your own healthcare. By taking an active role in your treatment, you can improve your overall health and well-being.

- How to advocate for your child's needs

Advocating for your child's needs is an essential skill that every parent should possess. As parents, it is our duty to ensure that our children receive the support and resources they require to thrive and succeed. Whether your child has special educational needs, medical conditions, or is facing challenges in school, advocating for them can make a significant difference in their lives. In this guide, we will discuss some key strategies and tips on how to effectively advocate for your child's needs.

The first step in advocating for your child is to educate yourself about their specific needs and challenges. Take the time to research their condition or diagnosis, understand their rights and entitlements, and familiarize yourself with relevant laws and policies. This knowledge will give you the confidence and information you need to effectively advocate for your child. Additionally, it is important to communicate with your child's doctors, teachers, therapists, and other professionals involved in their care to gain insights into their needs and develop a comprehensive understanding of their strengths and weaknesses.

Once you have a clear understanding of your child's needs, it is essential to establish clear goals and priorities for their care and support. Identify specific areas where your child requires assistance, such as academic accommodations, behavioral interventions, or medical treatments, and outline the steps needed to address these needs. Set achievable and realistic objectives that are tailored to your child's individual requirements and work collaboratively with professionals and educators to develop a customized plan to meet these goals.

Effective communication is key to successful advocacy. It is important to build positive and respectful relationships with the professionals and educators involved in your child's care. Keep an open line of communication and be an active participant in discussions about your child's needs. Clearly express your concerns, preferences, and expectations, and listen to the perspectives and recommendations of others. Collaborating with your child's team can lead to more effective solutions and support for your child's needs.

In advocating for your child, it is crucial to be proactive and persistent. Don't be afraid to speak up and assertively advocate for your child's rights and needs. Be prepared to ask questions, seek clarification, and advocate for changes or adjustments when necessary. Follow up on action plans and monitor progress towards your child's goals. Keep detailed records of conversations, agreements, and outcomes to ensure accountability and track your child's progress.

Another important aspect of advocating for your child is knowing your rights and entitlements. Familiarize yourself with relevant laws, regulations, and policies that protect and support children with special needs or disabilities. Be aware of your child's rights to accommodations, services, and support in educational settings, healthcare settings, and other areas of life. If you encounter challenges or barriers in accessing the resources your child needs, don't hesitate to seek guidance and support from advocacy organizations, legal experts, or other professionals who can help you navigate the system and advocate effectively for your child.

In advocating for your child, it is essential to prioritize their well-being and best interests above all else. Maintain a positive and empowering mindset, and approach advocacy with a sense of determination and resilience. Remember that you are your child's strongest advocate and champion, and your efforts can make a significant difference in their lives. By staying informed, communicating effectively, being proactive and persistent, knowing your rights, and prioritizing your child's needs, you can effectively advocate for your child and ensure they receive the support and resources they require to thrive and succeed.

Chapter 11: Promoting Healthy Lifestyle Choices

- Importance of healthy diet and exercise for children with ADHD

Attention-deficit/hyperactivity disorder (ADHD) is a neurodevelopmental disorder that affects numerous children worldwide. It is characterized by symptoms such as hyperactivity, impulsivity, and difficulties with attention and focus. While medication and therapy are common treatment options for managing ADHD symptoms, research has shown that a healthy diet and regular exercise can also play a crucial role in improving the overall well-being of children with ADHD. In this essay, we will explore the importance of a healthy diet and exercise for children with ADHD, how these lifestyle factors can impact symptoms, and practical tips for implementing them into a child's daily routine.

A well-balanced diet is essential for all children, but it is particularly important for those with ADHD. Research has shown that certain nutrients, such as omega-3 fatty acids, iron, zinc, and vitamins B6 and B12, can play a key role in supporting brain health and function, which is crucial for children with ADHD. Additionally, a diet rich in fruits, vegetables, whole grains, and lean proteins can help stabilize blood sugar levels, improve mood and energy levels, and reduce inflammation in the body. On the other hand, processed foods, sugary snacks, and foods high in artificial additives and preservatives have been linked to increased hyperactivity and impulsivity in children with ADHD. Therefore, adopting a diet that is high in nutrient-dense foods and low in processed foods and added sugars can help children with ADHD manage their symptoms more effectively.

In addition to a healthy diet, regular physical activity is also crucial for children with ADHD. Exercise has been shown to have numerous benefits for children with ADHD, including improved focus and attention, reduced hyperactivity and impulsivity, better mood regulation, and enhanced cognitive function. Physical activity helps stimulate the release of neurotransmitters such as dopamine and norepinephrine, which play a key role in regulating attention and focus. Furthermore, exercise can help reduce stress and anxiety, improve sleep quality, and boost self-esteem, all of which are important factors for children with ADHD. Encouraging children to engage in regular physical activity, whether it be through sports, dance, yoga, or simply playing outside, can have a significant impact on their overall well-being and symptom management.

When it comes to implementing a healthy diet and exercise routine for children with ADHD, there are several practical tips and strategies that parents and caregivers can consider. First and foremost, it is important to involve the child in meal planning and preparation, as this can help foster a sense of ownership and autonomy over their food choices. Encouraging children to try new foods and flavors, involving them in grocery shopping, and making mealtime a positive and enjoyable experience can help promote a healthy relationship with food. Additionally, setting a regular meal schedule and incorporating a variety of nutrient-dense foods into each meal can help stabilize blood sugar levels and support overall brain health.

In terms of exercise, it is important to find activities that the child enjoys and feels comfortable doing. Whether it be playing outside, participating in team sports, or practicing yoga or martial arts, finding a form of exercise that the child is enthusiastic about can help ensure that they stay active on a regular basis. Additionally, incorporating physical activity into the child's daily routine, such as walking or biking to school, taking active breaks throughout the day, and limiting screen time, can help promote a more active lifestyle. In summary, setting realistic and achievable goals for both diet and exercise, as well as providing positive reinforcement and praise for their efforts, can help motivate children with ADHD to stay committed to their health and wellness goals. By incorporating nutrient-dense foods, minimizing processed foods and added sugars, and promoting regular physical activity, parents and caregivers can help support their child's overall well-being and symptom management. Not only can a healthy diet and exercise routine improve focus and attention, reduce hyperactivity and impulsivity, and enhance mood and cognitive function, but they can also foster positive habits and behaviors that can benefit children with ADHD in the long run. By prioritizing nutrition and physical activity as part of a child's daily routine, we can help empower children with ADHD to thrive and reach their full potential.

- Strategies for promoting good sleep habits

Sleep is an essential component of our overall health and well-being. It is crucial for our physical, mental, and emotional health, as well as our ability to function effectively in our daily lives. However, many people struggle with sleep issues, whether it be difficulty falling asleep, staying asleep, or getting enough quality rest. Fortunately, there are several strategies that can be employed to promote good sleep habits and improve the quality of sleep.

One important strategy for promoting good sleep habits is to establish a consistent sleep schedule. This means going to bed and waking up at the same time every day, even on weekends. Our bodies have a natural internal clock, known as the circadian rhythm, that regulates our sleep-wake cycle. By sticking to a regular sleep schedule, we can help regulate our circadian rhythm and improve the quality of our sleep. Additionally, establishing a bedtime routine can signal to our bodies that it is time to wind down and prepare for sleep. This routine can include activities such as reading, taking a warm bath, or practicing relaxation techniques.

Another important strategy for promoting good sleep habits is to create a sleep-friendly environment. This means ensuring that your bedroom is a comfortable, quiet, and dark space that is conducive to sleep. Investing in a comfortable mattress and pillows, as well as using blackout curtains or a white noise machine, can help create an optimal sleep environment. It is also important to keep your bedroom at a cool temperature, as cooler temperatures are typically more conducive to sleep. Additionally, limiting screen time before bedtime and turning off electronic devices at least an hour before bed can help signal to your body that it is time to wind down and prepare for sleep.

In addition to establishing a consistent sleep schedule and creating a sleep-friendly environment, practicing good sleep hygiene is also important for promoting good sleep habits. This includes avoiding stimulants such as caffeine and nicotine close to bedtime, as well as limiting alcohol consumption, which can disrupt sleep. It is also important to avoid heavy meals close to bedtime, as well as to engage in regular exercise, which can promote better sleep. Additionally, practicing relaxation techniques such as deep breathing, progressive muscle relaxation, or meditation can help reduce stress and prepare your body for sleep.

For those who continue to struggle with sleep issues despite implementing these strategies, it may be helpful to speak with a healthcare professional. There are several potential underlying medical conditions that can contribute to sleep problems, such as sleep apnea, restless leg syndrome, or insomnia. A healthcare professional can help diagnose and treat these conditions, as well as provide guidance on additional strategies for improving sleep. In some cases, a sleep study may be recommended to further evaluate any potential sleep disorders. By establishing a consistent sleep schedule, creating a sleep-friendly environment, practicing good sleep hygiene, and seeking help from a healthcare professional if necessary, individuals can improve the quality of their sleep and enhance their overall quality of life. Prioritizing sleep and making it a priority in our daily routines can have a profound impact on our physical, mental, and emotional health. By taking action to promote good sleep habits, we can improve our quality of life and enjoy the benefits of restful, rejuvenating sleep.

- Managing screen time and technology usage

In today's digital age, managing screen time and technology usage has become a pressing issue for individuals of all ages. The increasing prevalence of smartphones, tablets, computers, and other devices has led to a significant rise in the amount of time people spend in front of screens. While technology has undoubtedly revolutionized the way we communicate, work, and entertain ourselves, excessive screen time can have detrimental effects on our physical and mental well-being. It is therefore essential to establish healthy habits and boundaries when it comes to using technology, in order to maintain a balanced and fulfilling lifestyle.

One of the key reasons why managing screen time is important is the impact it can have on our physical health. Prolonged exposure to screens can lead to a range of health issues, including eye strain, headaches, and neck and back pain. The blue light emitted by screens can disrupt our sleep patterns, leading to fatigue and irritability. Additionally, excessive screen time has been linked to an increased risk of obesity, as it often leads to a sedentary lifestyle and poor dietary habits. By implementing guidelines for screen time, such as taking regular breaks, practicing good posture, and setting limits on usage, individuals can reduce their risk of developing these health issues and improve their overall well-being.

In addition to physical health concerns, managing screen time is also crucial for maintaining our mental health. Studies have shown that excessive screen time can contribute to feelings of stress, anxiety, and depression. Constant exposure to social media and other online platforms can lead to negative self-comparisons, feelings of inadequacy, and a distorted sense of reality. Furthermore, the constant barrage of notifications, messages, and alerts can be overwhelming and disrupt our ability to focus and concentrate. By establishing boundaries for technology usage, such as turning off notifications, setting aside designated screen-free time, and engaging in offline activities, individuals can protect their mental health and cultivate a sense of well-being.

Another important consideration when it comes to managing screen time is its impact on our relationships and social interactions. Excessive use of technology can lead to a decline in face-to-face communication, as well as a decrease in the quality of our relationships. Constantly checking our phones or devices during conversations can be perceived as rude or disinterested, and can erode the bonds we have with others. Additionally, spending too much time on social media or online platforms can create a false sense of connection, as it often lacks the depth and intimacy of real-world interactions. By setting boundaries around technology usage, such as establishing device-free zones in the home, prioritizing in-person interactions, and engaging in meaningful activities with loved ones, individuals can nurture their relationships and strengthen their social connections.

Furthermore, managing screen time is essential for promoting cognitive development and mental acuity. Excessive use of technology has been associated with a decline in attention span, memory, and critical thinking skills. Constantly switching between tasks and being bombarded with information can overload our brains and impede our ability to process and retain new information. By limiting screen time and engaging in activities that require focus, concentration, and problem-solving, individuals can sharpen their cognitive abilities and enhance their mental agility. Additionally, setting aside time for activities such as reading, hobbies, and creative pursuits can stimulate the brain and foster personal growth and development. By implementing strategies to limit screen time, establish boundaries, and prioritize offline activities, individuals can protect their physical and mental well-being, nurture their relationships, and enhance their cognitive abilities. While technology has the power to enrich our lives and connect us with others, it is essential to use it mindfully and intentionally in order to reap its benefits while minimizing its potential negative effects. By taking control of our screen time, we can create a more fulfilling and harmonious relationship with technology and cultivate a greater sense of well-being in our daily lives.

Chapter 12: Handling Challenging Behaviors

- Strategies for managing aggression and defiance

Aggression and defiance are common behaviors in both children and adults that can cause disruptive and challenging situations in various settings, including schools, workplaces, and homes. It is essential to have effective strategies in place to manage and address these behaviors in a way that is constructive and promotes positive outcomes for all involved. By understanding the underlying causes of aggression and defiance, as well as implementing appropriate interventions and techniques, individuals can learn to regulate their emotions and behaviors more effectively.

One of the key factors to consider when managing aggression and defiance is understanding the root causes of these behaviors. Aggression and defiance can stem from a variety of factors, including stress, trauma, underlying mental health issues, and ineffective communication skills. By identifying the specific triggers and underlying issues that contribute to these behaviors, individuals can develop targeted interventions that address the root cause and promote more positive and adaptive responses. This requires a comprehensive understanding of the individual's unique challenges and needs, as well as a collaborative approach that involves input from the individual, their support system, and relevant professionals.

In addition to understanding the underlying causes of aggression and defiance, it is essential to implement effective interventions and strategies to address these behaviors in a proactive and supportive manner. One effective strategy is to establish clear boundaries and expectations for behavior, and consistently reinforce these expectations through positive reinforcement and appropriate consequences. By setting clear and consistent guidelines for behavior, individuals can learn to regulate their emotions and responses more effectively, reducing the likelihood of aggressive or defiant behaviors occurring. It is also important to provide individuals with alternative coping skills and strategies to manage their emotions and impulses in a healthy and constructive way. This may include teaching individuals relaxation techniques, communication skills, problem-solving strategies, and anger management techniques.

Another important aspect of managing aggression and defiance is promoting a positive and supportive environment that fosters healthy relationships and communication. Building strong relationships based on trust, respect, and understanding can help individuals feel safe and supported, reducing the likelihood of engaging in aggressive or defiant behaviors. By promoting open and honest communication, individuals can express their thoughts and feelings in a constructive way, rather than resorting to aggressive or defiant behaviors as a means of communicating their needs. It is also crucial to provide individuals with opportunities for social and emotional learning, such as peer mediation programs, conflict resolution training, and social skills development, to help them build positive relationships and develop effective communication skills. By promoting a positive and supportive environment, establishing clear boundaries and expectations, and providing individuals with alternative coping skills and communication strategies, individuals can learn to regulate their emotions and behaviors more effectively, reducing the likelihood of engaging in aggressive or defiant behaviors. With a collaborative and empathetic approach, individuals can develop the skills and resilience needed to overcome their challenges and build healthier and more fulfilling relationships.

- Tips for dealing with meltdowns and tantrums

When it comes to dealing with meltdowns and tantrums, it's important to understand that these behaviors are a natural part of child development. Children are still learning how to regulate their emotions and communicate effectively, so it's normal for them to experience strong emotions and have difficulty expressing them in a constructive way. As parents and caregivers, it's our job to help guide them through these challenging moments with patience and compassion.

One tip for dealing with meltdowns and tantrums is to try to prevent them from occurring in the first place. This can be done by setting clear expectations and boundaries for your child, and providing them with a consistent routine and structure. Children thrive on predictability, so having a schedule in place can help them feel more secure and less likely to act out. It's also important to make sure your child is well-rested and well-fed, as hunger and tiredness can exacerbate emotional outbursts.

When a meltdown or tantrum does occur, it's important to stay calm and composed. It can be difficult to remain level-headed when your child is screaming and crying, but getting angry or lashing out will only escalate the situation. Take a deep breath and remind yourself that your child is struggling, and that they need your help and support. Try to validate their feelings and let them know that it's okay to be upset, but also set boundaries and let them know that their behavior is not acceptable.

One effective strategy for dealing with meltdowns and tantrums is to use positive reinforcement. This involves praising and rewarding your child for good behavior, rather than focusing on their negative behavior. When your child is able to calm down and express their emotions in a more appropriate way, make sure to acknowledge their efforts and offer praise. This will help reinforce positive behaviors and encourage your child to continue making good choices in the future.

It's also important to teach your child healthy coping mechanisms for dealing with strong emotions. Encourage them to take deep breaths, count to ten, or use a calming technique like a stress ball or fidget spinner. Help them identify their feelings and talk about what is causing them to feel upset. By empowering your child to understand and manage their emotions, you can help them develop important skills that will serve them well throughout their lives.

In some cases, meltdowns and tantrums may be a sign of an underlying issue, such as anxiety, sensory processing disorder, or ADHD. If you notice that your child is having frequent or severe meltdowns, it may be helpful to consult with a pediatrician or mental health professional for further evaluation and support. They can provide valuable insights and strategies for addressing your child's specific needs, and help you develop a plan for managing challenging behaviors in a more effective way. By setting clear expectations, staying calm in the face of emotional outbursts, using positive reinforcement, teaching healthy coping mechanisms, and seeking professional support when needed, you can create a supportive environment for your child to thrive and develop important social and emotional skills. Remember, every child is unique, and it's important to tailor your approach to meet their individual needs and strengths. With time and consistency, you can help your child navigate meltdowns and tantrums with grace and resilience.

- Importance of staying calm and patient

In today's fast-paced and ever-changing world, the ability to stay calm and patient is more important than ever. Whether it be dealing with daily stressors, navigating challenging situations, or facing unexpected obstacles, staying calm and patient can greatly enhance our ability to think clearly, make rational decisions, and maintain a sense of well-being. In this discussion, we will explore the importance of staying calm and patient in various aspects of our personal and professional lives, and provide tips on how to cultivate these valuable qualities.

One of the key benefits of staying calm and patient is the enhanced ability to deal with stress and adversity. In our modern society, we are constantly bombarded with deadlines, commitments, and pressures that can easily overwhelm us if we allow them to. By remaining calm and patient in the face of stress, we are better equipped to handle challenges, problem-solve effectively, and maintain a positive mindset. This can lead to improved resilience, emotional stability, and overall well-being.

Additionally, staying calm and patient can improve our relationships with others. When we are able to remain composed and level-headed in difficult situations, we are more likely to communicate effectively, show empathy, and demonstrate understanding towards others. This can lead to stronger interpersonal connections, enhanced collaboration, and a more harmonious work environment. By practicing patience and maintaining a sense of calm, we can foster positive relationships and create a supportive and inclusive community.

Furthermore, staying calm and patient can have a positive impact on our productivity and performance. When we are able to maintain a sense of composure and focus, we are better able to concentrate on tasks, manage our time effectively, and execute our responsibilities with precision and excellence. This can lead to improved efficiency, higher quality work, and increased satisfaction with our accomplishments. By staying calm and patient, we can cultivate a sense of mindfulness and intentionality in our actions, leading to greater productivity and success in our endeavors.

In addition to its benefits in personal and professional realms, staying calm and patient also plays a crucial role in promoting mental and emotional well-being. In today's fast-paced and high-stress society, the ability to remain calm and patient can help us navigate our emotions, manage our reactions, and cultivate a sense of inner peace and tranquility. By adopting a patient and composed attitude, we can learn to regulate our emotions, cope with challenges, and maintain a positive outlook on life. This can lead to improved mental health, reduced anxiety, and greater overall happiness and fulfillment.

To cultivate a sense of calm and patience in our lives, there are several strategies that we can implement. One key practice is mindfulness meditation, which involves focusing on the present moment and observing our thoughts and emotions without judgment. By engaging in regular mindfulness meditation, we can cultivate a sense of awareness and self-control, which can help us stay calm and patient in challenging situations. Additionally, practicing deep breathing exercises, taking breaks to relax and recharge, and engaging in activities that bring us joy and fulfillment can also help us maintain a sense of calm and patience. In today's fast-paced and high-stress world, maintaining a sense of composure, patience, and resilience is essential for navigating the challenges and uncertainties that life throws our way. By cultivating these valuable qualities, we can enhance our ability to deal with stress, build strong relationships, improve our productivity and performance, and promote mental and emotional well-being. By adopting mindfulness practices, engaging in relaxation techniques, and finding activities that bring us joy and fulfillment, we can empower ourselves to stay calm and patient in the face of adversity, and lead a more fulfilling and balanced life.

Chapter 13: Balancing Discipline and Empathy

- Importance of setting limits and boundaries

Setting limits and boundaries is a crucial aspect of maintaining healthy relationships and ensuring personal well-being. Whether in professional or personal contexts, boundaries define the acceptable behaviors and interactions that individuals are comfortable with. Without clear boundaries, people may feel overwhelmed, disrespected, or taken advantage of. Establishing limits helps to protect one's physical, emotional, and mental health, as well as fostering mutual respect and understanding in relationships.

In professional settings, setting boundaries is essential for maintaining professionalism and productivity. For instance, clearly defined boundaries can prevent overwork and burnout by ensuring that individuals have time for rest and self-care. It also helps to prevent conflicts and misunderstandings that may arise from unclear expectations. By establishing boundaries, employees can communicate their needs and limitations to their supervisors and colleagues, which can lead to a more harmonious work environment.

On the other hand, in personal relationships, boundaries play a vital role in fostering healthy dynamics and mutual respect. When individuals set boundaries, they communicate their values, needs, and limits to others, which helps to prevent feelings of resentment or disrespect. Boundaries also help to safeguard one's emotional well-being by ensuring that individuals are not subjected to harmful or toxic behaviors from others. By setting limits, individuals can protect themselves from manipulation, coercion, or abuse in relationships.

Moreover, setting boundaries is an act of self-care and self-respect. By establishing limits, individuals assert their autonomy and assert their right to be treated with dignity and respect. It also helps to build self-esteem and confidence by affirming one's worth and value. Additionally, setting boundaries allows individuals to prioritize their well-being and ensure that their needs are met, which is essential for maintaining a healthy and balanced life.

Setting limits and boundaries is not about being rigid or controlling; instead, it is about setting clear expectations and communicating them effectively. It is important to remember that boundaries are not set in stone and can be adjusted as needed. Flexibility is key when it comes to establishing boundaries, as situations and relationships may change over time. By maintaining open lines of communication and being willing to reassess boundaries when necessary, individuals can ensure that their limits are respected and their well-being is protected. By establishing clear boundaries, individuals can protect themselves from harm, communicate their needs effectively, and foster mutual respect in relationships. Whether in professional or personal contexts, boundaries are essential for creating a safe and supportive environment where individuals can thrive and grow. By prioritizing self-care, self-respect, and clear communication, individuals can establish boundaries that promote their well-being and ensure that their needs are met.

- Strategies for disciplining children with ADHD

ADHD, or Attention-Deficit/Hyperactivity Disorder, is a neurodevelopmental disorder that affects the way children process information and regulate their behavior. Children with ADHD may struggle with paying attention, sitting still, and controlling their impulses, which can make traditional discipline strategies less effective. However, with the right approach, parents and caregivers can help children with ADHD learn to manage their behavior and develop positive habits.

One effective strategy for disciplining children with ADHD is to set clear and consistent expectations. Children with ADHD thrive on routine and structure, so it is important to establish clear rules and consequences for their behavior. Make sure your expectations are age-appropriate and realistic, and be consistent in enforcing them. Children with ADHD may have trouble remembering and following rules, so providing reminders and visual cues can be helpful.

Another important strategy for disciplining children with ADHD is to use positive reinforcement. Children with ADHD respond well to praise and rewards for good behavior, so be sure to acknowledge and celebrate their successes. This can help build their self-esteem and motivate them to continue making positive choices. It is also important to focus on the positive aspects of their behavior, rather than constantly pointing out their mistakes.

In addition to providing positive reinforcement, it is important to use consequences effectively when disciplining children with ADHD. Consequences should be meaningful and appropriate for the behavior, and should be given in a calm and consistent manner. It is important to avoid harsh or punitive consequences, as this can be counterproductive and may damage the child's self-esteem. Instead, focus on natural consequences and logical consequences that help the child learn from their actions.

It is also important to consider the child's individual needs and preferences when developing discipline strategies. Children with ADHD may have different sensory sensitivities, communication styles, and learning preferences, so it is important to tailor your approach to meet their unique needs. For example, some children with ADHD may respond well to visual schedules and checklists, while others may prefer hands-on activities and movement breaks. By understanding your child's strengths and challenges, you can develop discipline strategies that are effective and empowering.

Furthermore, it is important to collaborate with teachers, therapists, and other professionals to develop a comprehensive approach to discipline for children with ADHD. Working together with a team of experts can help ensure that your child receives the support and guidance they need to succeed. This may involve developing a behavior plan, setting up accommodations in the classroom, or seeking additional therapies and interventions to support your child's social and emotional development.

To summarize, it is important to practice self-care and patience when disciplining children with ADHD. Parenting a child with ADHD can be challenging and stressful at times, so it is important to take care of yourself and seek support when needed. Remember that progress takes time, and that it is normal to experience setbacks along the way. By practicing self-compassion and staying committed to your child's well-being, you can help them develop the skills and habits they need to thrive.

- How to show empathy and understanding

Empathy and understanding are essential components of successful communication and relationships, both in professional settings and personal interactions. Showing empathy and understanding involves recognizing and acknowledging the emotions and perspectives of others, and responding in a way that demonstrates care and consideration for their feelings. In this guide, we will explore some strategies and techniques for effectively showing empathy and understanding in various contexts.

One important aspect of showing empathy and understanding is active listening. This means giving the speaker your full attention, making eye contact, and responding appropriately to what they are saying. It involves not only hearing the words that are spoken, but also paying attention to nonverbal cues such as body language and facial expressions. Reflective listening is a technique that can help demonstrate empathy, by paraphrasing or summarizing what the speaker has said to show that you are truly engaged and understanding their perspective.

Another key element of showing empathy and understanding is being open-minded and non-judgmental. It is important to set aside your own assumptions and biases, and approach the situation with an open heart and mind. Try to put yourself in the other person's shoes, and consider how they might be feeling or what they might be going through. Avoid jumping to s or making assumptions about their emotions or motivations, and instead focus on truly understanding their perspective and experiences.

Empathy and understanding also involve expressing genuine care and concern for the well-being of others. This can be done through verbal expressions of empathy, such as saying things like "I understand how you must be feeling" or "I sympathize with what you're going through. " It can also be shown through nonverbal cues, such as a comforting touch or a reassuring smile. Letting the other person know that you are there for them and that you care about their feelings can go a long way in building trust and strengthening your relationship with them.

In addition to actively listening and expressing care and concern, showing empathy and understanding also involves validating the other person's emotions and experiences. This means acknowledging and accepting their feelings as valid, even if you may not agree with them or fully understand them. Avoid dismissing or minimizing their emotions, and instead validate their feelings by saying things like "I can see why you would feel that way" or "It's okay to feel upset about this. " Validating someone's emotions can help them feel heard and understood, and can foster a sense of trust and connection in your relationship.

In brief, showing empathy and understanding also requires being patient and giving the other person space to express themselves. It is important to allow the other person to share their thoughts and feelings at their own pace, without rushing them or interrupting them. Giving them the time and space they need to communicate can help them feel heard and respected, and can create a safe and supportive environment for them to open up and share their emotions. Patience is key in showing empathy and understanding, as it allows the other person to feel valued and appreciated for who they are and what they are going through. By actively listening, being open-minded and non-judgmental, expressing care and concern, validating others' emotions, and being patient and giving them space to communicate, you can demonstrate empathy and understanding in a meaningful and effective way. By cultivating these skills and techniques, you can strengthen your relationships, improve your communication skills, and create a more supportive and empathetic environment for yourself and those around you.

Chapter 14: Strengthening Parent-Child Relationships

- Importance of building a strong bond with your child

Building a strong bond with your child is crucial for their overall well-being and development. Research studies have shown that children who have secure attachments with their parents are more likely to thrive academically, socially, and emotionally. When a child feels loved, supported, and understood by their parents, they are more likely to have higher levels of self-esteem and confidence. This strong bond also helps children develop healthy relationships with others, as they learn how to trust and communicate effectively.

One of the key benefits of building a strong bond with your child is the impact it has on their mental health. Children who have a secure attachment with their parents are better able to regulate their emotions and cope with stress. They are also less likely to develop anxiety or depression later in life. By providing a safe and loving environment for your child, you are helping them develop the skills and resilience they need to navigate life's challenges.

In addition to the emotional benefits, building a strong bond with your child also has positive effects on their cognitive development. Children who feel secure in their relationships with their parents are more likely to feel confident in exploring their environment and trying new things. This sense of security and confidence allows them to learn and grow at their own pace, which in turn, can lead to higher academic achievement. By nurturing a strong bond with your child, you are helping them develop a love for learning and a curiosity about the world around them.

Furthermore, building a strong bond with your child can have a significant impact on their behavior. Children who feel connected to their parents are more likely to follow rules and guidelines set by their caregivers. They are also more likely to exhibit prosocial behaviors, such as kindness and empathy towards others. By fostering a strong bond with your child, you are teaching them important values and morals that will shape their behavior and decision-making as they grow older.

It is important to note that building a strong bond with your child is not solely about spending time together or providing for their physical needs. It also requires emotional availability, empathy, and the ability to truly listen and understand your child's thoughts and feelings. When a child feels heard and validated by their parents, it strengthens the bond between them and creates a sense of trust and safety. By providing a secure and loving relationship, you are equipping your child with the tools and skills they need to thrive in all aspects of their life. So take the time to connect with your child on a deeper level, listen to their needs, and show them that you are there for them unconditionally. Your efforts will pay off in the long run, as you watch your child grow into a confident, resilient, and compassionate individual.

- Tips for enhancing communication and connection

Effective communication is a fundamental aspect of human interaction that plays a crucial role in fostering relationships and building connections with others. Whether in personal relationships, professional settings, or social interactions, the ability to communicate effectively is essential for expressing thoughts, ideas, and emotions, as well as for understanding and empathizing with others. In order to enhance communication and connection with others, there are several tips and strategies that can be followed to improve the quality of interaction and strengthen relationships.

One key tip for enhancing communication and connection is to actively listen to others. Listening is a vital component of effective communication, as it demonstrates respect, empathy, and understanding towards the speaker. By paying attention to what the other person is saying, one can show genuine interest in their thoughts and feelings, which can help to create a sense of connection and rapport. Active listening involves focusing on the speaker, avoiding interruptions, and providing feedback through verbal and nonverbal cues to indicate understanding and engagement. By practicing active listening, individuals can improve their communication skills and deepen their connections with others.

Another tip for enhancing communication and connection is to be mindful of nonverbal communication cues. Nonverbal communication, such as body language, facial expressions, and tone of voice, plays a significant role in conveying messages and emotions in interpersonal interactions. Being aware of one's own nonverbal cues and being attentive to the nonverbal cues of others can help to enhance communication and establish a stronger connection with others. For example, maintaining eye contact, using open body language, and mirroring the nonverbal cues of the speaker can signal attentiveness, empathy, and receptiveness, which can foster a sense of trust and understanding in the conversation.

In addition to active listening and nonverbal communication, another tip for enhancing communication and connection is to practice empathy and understanding. Empathy is the ability to understand and share the feelings of others, and it plays a crucial role in building connections and fostering positive relationships. By putting oneself in the shoes of the other person and seeing things from their perspective, one can develop a deeper understanding of their thoughts, emotions, and experiences, which can lead to greater empathy, trust, and connection. By showing empathy and understanding towards others, individuals can create a supportive and nurturing environment for communication, where feelings are validated, and connections are strengthened.

Furthermore, another tip for enhancing communication and connection is to be clear and concise in one's communication. Clear and concise communication involves expressing thoughts, ideas, and feelings in a straightforward and easy-to-understand manner, which can prevent misunderstandings, confusion, and misinterpretation in conversations. By using simple language, organizing thoughts effectively, and avoiding jargon or unnecessary detail, individuals can communicate more effectively and convey their message clearly to the other person. Clear and concise communication can help to facilitate understanding, promote engagement, and strengthen connections in interpersonal interactions.

Moreover, another tip for enhancing communication and connection is to practice assertiveness and self-expression. Assertiveness is the ability to express one's thoughts, feelings, and needs in a respectful and confident manner, without being passive or aggressive. By being assertive in communication, individuals can assert their boundaries, express their opinions, and advocate for their needs, which can enhance self-esteem, promote authenticity, and create a sense of trust and respect in relationships. Assertive communication involves speaking up for oneself, standing up for what one believes in, and expressing views honestly and openly, which can foster mutual understanding and connection in interactions. By following the tips and strategies mentioned above, individuals can enhance their communication skills, deepen their connections with others, and create a supportive and nurturing environment for interaction. Active listening, mindfulness of nonverbal cues, empathy and understanding, clear and concise communication, and assertiveness and self-expression are key components of effective communication that can help to improve engagement, understanding, and connection in interpersonal interactions. By practicing these tips and strategies, individuals can enhance their communication and connection with others, foster positive relationships, and create meaningful connections that enrich their personal and professional lives.

- Ways to nurture a positive parent-child relationship

Parent-child relationships are foundational to a child's development and overall well-being. Nurturing a positive parent-child relationship involves building a strong emotional connection, fostering open communication, setting boundaries, and providing support and guidance. This relationship lays the groundwork for a child's social, emotional, and cognitive development, and can have a lasting impact on their future relationships and success in life.

One of the key ways to nurture a positive parent-child relationship is through building a strong emotional connection. This involves showing love and affection, spending quality time together, and being present and attentive to your child's needs. It is important for parents to create a secure attachment with their child, as this lays the foundation for their emotional and social development. By responding to their child's needs with warmth and empathy, parents can create a sense of security and trust that will help their child feel safe and supported.

Open communication is another essential component of a positive parent-child relationship. Parents should encourage their child to express their thoughts, feelings, and concerns openly and honestly. By listening actively and attentively to their child, parents can show that they value their opinions and feelings, and are willing to support and validate them. It is important for parents to create a safe and non-judgmental environment where their child feels comfortable sharing their thoughts and emotions. By fostering open communication, parents can strengthen their relationship with their child and build a greater sense of trust and understanding between them.

Setting boundaries is also crucial in nurturing a positive parent-child relationship. Boundaries help children understand expectations, develop self-discipline, and learn to respect themselves and others. Parents should establish clear and consistent rules and consequences, and enforce them in a fair and consistent manner. It is important for parents to set boundaries that are age-appropriate and consistent with their child's developmental stage. By setting boundaries, parents can help their child understand limits, develop self-control, and learn to navigate the world in a safe and responsible manner.

Providing support and guidance is another key aspect of nurturing a positive parent-child relationship. Parents should be there to support their child through the ups and downs of life, and offer guidance and encouragement when needed. By being a positive role model and offering words of wisdom and advice, parents can help their child navigate challenges and develop the skills and resilience they need to thrive. It is important for parents to be patient, compassionate, and understanding, and to provide a listening ear and a shoulder to lean on when their child needs it most. By focusing on these key elements, parents can create a loving, supportive, and nurturing environment for their child to grow and thrive. A positive parent-child relationship is essential for a child's emotional, social, and cognitive development, and can have a lasting impact on their well-being and success in life. By investing time and effort into building a positive relationship with their child, parents can help them develop the skills and resilience they need to lead happy, healthy, and fulfilling lives.

Chapter 15: Fostering Independence and Autonomy

- Strategies for promoting independence in children with ADHD

Attention Deficit Hyperactivity Disorder (ADHD) is a neurodevelopmental disorder that affects individuals' ability to focus, control impulses, and regulate behavior. Children with ADHD may struggle with tasks that require sustained attention, organization, and self-regulation. This can impact their ability to be independent in various aspects of their lives, such as completing homework, managing their time, and making decisions. However, there are strategies that parents, educators, and other caregivers can implement to promote independence in children with ADHD.

One key strategy for promoting independence in children with ADHD is to provide structure and routine. Establishing predictable schedules and clear expectations can help children with ADHD feel more organized and in control of their environment. This can include creating a daily routine that includes set times for activities such as homework, meals, and bedtime. Breaking tasks down into smaller, manageable steps can also help children with ADHD feel less overwhelmed and more capable of completing tasks independently.

Another important strategy for promoting independence in children with ADHD is to provide ongoing support and guidance. Children with ADHD may struggle with initiating tasks, staying focused, and staying organized. Providing gentle reminders, positive reinforcement, and praise for small accomplishments can help children with ADHD build confidence and develop the skills necessary to be independent. Additionally, teaching children with ADHD strategies for self-regulation, such as deep breathing exercises or mindfulness techniques, can help them manage their impulsivity and stay focused on tasks.

It is also important to encourage children with ADHD to develop self-advocacy skills. Teaching children how to communicate their needs and preferences to teachers, peers, and other adults can help them advocate for themselves and make their own decisions. This can involve role-playing scenarios where children practice asking for help or accommodations, as well as teaching them how to use tools such as checklists or visual schedules to help them stay organized and on track.

In addition to providing support and guidance, it is important to create a positive and supportive environment for children with ADHD. Children with ADHD may face stigma, judgment, and discrimination, which can impact their self-esteem and confidence. By creating a safe and inclusive environment where children feel accepted and supported, caregivers can help children with ADHD develop a sense of belonging and self-worth. This can involve promoting a growth mindset, where children are encouraged to see challenges as opportunities for growth and learning, rather than as failures.

Collaborating with educators, healthcare providers, and other professionals can also be beneficial in promoting independence in children with ADHD. By working together, caregivers can gain valuable insights and resources to support children with ADHD in school, at home, and in the community. This can involve developing individualized education plans, collaborating on behavior management strategies, and seeking out additional support services such as tutoring or therapy.

Ultimately, promoting independence in children with ADHD requires patience, flexibility, and understanding. Children with ADHD may have unique needs and challenges, but with the right support and strategies in place, they can develop the skills and confidence necessary to be independent and successful. By providing structure, support, and encouragement, caregivers can help children with ADHD thrive and reach their full potential.

- Tips for teaching self-care and responsibility

Self-care and responsibility are essential components of a healthy and fulfilling life. Teaching these concepts to others, whether it be in a classroom setting, a workplace environment, or simply to friends and family, can have a profound impact on their well-being. In this article, we will discuss some tips for effectively teaching self-care and responsibility, and how to encourage others to prioritize these aspects of their lives.

One of the first steps in teaching self-care and responsibility is to lead by example. It is important to practice what you preach and demonstrate to others the importance of taking care of oneself and fulfilling obligations. By showing that you prioritize self-care and responsibility in your own life, you can inspire those around you to do the same. This can be as simple as setting boundaries and taking time for yourself, or as complex as consistently meeting deadlines and fulfilling commitments.

Another key aspect of teaching self-care and responsibility is to provide education and resources to others. This can involve sharing information about the benefits of self-care, such as improved mental and physical health, increased productivity, and better relationships. It can also involve offering tips and strategies for incorporating self-care into daily life, such as exercise, meditation, journaling, and setting goals. By equipping others with the knowledge and tools they need to prioritize self-care and responsibility, you empower them to take control of their own well-being.

In addition to leading by example and providing education and resources, it is important to create a supportive and encouraging environment for those you are teaching. This can involve offering positive reinforcement when individuals engage in self-care activities or fulfill their responsibilities, as well as providing constructive feedback and guidance when they struggle. It is important to foster a sense of empathy and understanding, and to show that you care about the well-being of those you are teaching. By creating a supportive and encouraging environment, you can help others feel motivated and empowered to prioritize self-care and responsibility.

It is also important to tailor your teaching approach to the individual needs and preferences of those you are teaching. Everyone is different, and what works for one person may not work for another. It is important to take the time to get to know the people you are teaching, and to understand their unique strengths, challenges, and goals. By taking a personalized approach to teaching self-care and responsibility, you can help individuals develop strategies that work for them and that fit into their lifestyle.

Lastly, it is important to emphasize the importance of self-compassion and forgiveness in teaching self-care and responsibility. It is inevitable that individuals will make mistakes or fall short of their goals from time to time. It is important to remind them that it is okay to not be perfect, and to show them how to learn from their mistakes and move forward with a sense of resilience and determination. By emphasizing self-compassion and forgiveness, you can help individuals develop a healthy and balanced approach to self-care and responsibility. By leading by example, providing education and resources, creating a supportive and encouraging environment, tailoring your teaching approach to individual needs, and emphasizing self-compassion and forgiveness, you can help others develop the skills and mindset they need to prioritize self-care and responsibility in their lives. With your guidance and support, you can inspire those around you to lead healthier, more fulfilling lives.

- Importance of allowing children to make choices

Allowing children to make choices is crucial in their development and growth. When children are able to make their own decisions, they learn to take responsibility for their actions and develop critical thinking skills. By giving children the opportunity to make choices, they are able to build confidence and self-esteem as they see the impact of their decisions on their lives.

Furthermore, allowing children to make choices fosters a sense of agency and empowerment. When children are able to make decisions for themselves, they feel like they have a say in their own lives and are more likely to take ownership of their actions. This sense of agency can translate into other areas of their lives, such as in their relationships with peers and adults. By giving children the freedom to make choices, we are teaching them that their thoughts and opinions matter, and that they have the power to shape their own future.

In addition, allowing children to make choices helps to develop their decision-making skills. Decision-making is a critical skill that children will need throughout their lives, and the more practice they have in making choices, the better equipped they will be to navigate the complexities of the world. By allowing children to make decisions, we are helping them learn how to weigh options, consider consequences, and make informed choices. These skills are essential for success in school, work, and life in general.

Moreover, allowing children to make choices can also help them develop a sense of identity and values. When children are able to make decisions based on their own preferences and beliefs, they are able to better understand who they are as individuals. This self-awareness is crucial for building a strong sense of self and developing a sense of direction in life. By allowing children to make choices, we are helping them explore their interests and passions, and develop a strong sense of self-worth.

It is important to note that allowing children to make choices does not mean giving them free rein to do whatever they want. It is essential for adults to set boundaries and provide guidance to ensure that children are making safe and healthy choices. By offering children a balance of freedom and structure, we can help them learn to make responsible decisions while still empowering them to take control of their own lives. By giving children the freedom to make decisions, we are helping them build confidence, develop critical thinking skills, foster a sense of agency and empowerment, and learn important decision-making skills. By allowing children to make choices, we are helping them develop a strong sense of identity and values, and teaching them the importance of taking responsibility for their actions.

Chapter 16: Coping with Everyday Challenges

- Strategies for managing everyday tasks and responsibilities

Managing everyday tasks and responsibilities can sometimes feel overwhelming, but with the right strategies in place, it is possible to stay organized and on top of everything. One key strategy is creating a daily to-do list. This simple practice can help you prioritize your tasks and focus on what needs to be done each day. Start by listing out all of the tasks you need to accomplish, then prioritize them based on importance and deadline. By breaking down your to-do list into smaller, more manageable tasks, you can avoid feeling overwhelmed and ensure that everything gets done in a timely manner.

Another important strategy for managing everyday tasks and responsibilities is time blocking. This involves setting aside specific blocks of time for different tasks or activities throughout the day. By allocating dedicated time slots for tasks like checking emails, working on projects, and taking breaks, you can prevent distractions and stay focused on the task at hand. Time blocking can also help you balance your workload and ensure that you are not neglecting important tasks or responsibilities.

In addition to creating a to-do list and time blocking, it is important to establish a routine that works for you. By developing a daily routine, you can create structure and consistency in your day, which can help you stay motivated and productive. Start by identifying your peak productivity hours and scheduling your most important tasks during that time. This will allow you to make the most of your energy and focus on tasks that require your full attention. Additionally, incorporating healthy habits like regular exercise, adequate sleep, and proper nutrition into your routine can help you maintain your physical and mental wellbeing, which can in turn improve your productivity and ability to manage everyday tasks and responsibilities.

Another effective strategy for managing everyday tasks and responsibilities is setting realistic goals. By breaking down larger projects or responsibilities into smaller, manageable goals, you can stay on track and make progress towards completing them. Set specific, measurable, achievable, relevant, and time-bound (SMART) goals for each task or project, and track your progress regularly to ensure that you are moving forward. Celebrate small victories along the way to stay motivated and build momentum towards achieving your larger goals. By setting realistic goals and holding yourself accountable, you can avoid procrastination and ensure that you are making steady progress towards completing your tasks and responsibilities.

One final strategy for managing everyday tasks and responsibilities is delegating when necessary. It is important to recognize when you are feeling overwhelmed or when certain tasks could be completed more efficiently by someone else. Look for opportunities to delegate tasks to colleagues, family members, or professionals who can help lighten your workload and allow you to focus on more important priorities. By delegating tasks effectively, you can free up time and energy for tasks that require your expertise and attention, ultimately increasing your productivity and ability to manage your responsibilities effectively. By implementing these strategies into your daily routine, you can stay organized, focused, and productive, while also maintaining a healthy work-life balance. Remember to be flexible and adaptable in your approach, as what works for one person may not work for another. Experiment with different strategies and techniques until you find what works best for you, and don't be afraid to seek help or support when needed. With the right strategies in place, you can successfully manage your everyday tasks and responsibilities with confidence and ease.

- Tips for dealing with transitions and changes

Transitions and changes are an inevitable part of life, whether they are personal or professional. While they can be challenging and even overwhelming at times, there are strategies that can help individuals navigate these periods of transition with greater ease and resilience. In this article, we will discuss some tips for dealing with transitions and changes, drawing on psychological research and practical advice to offer a comprehensive guide for managing these transitions effectively.

One of the key strategies for dealing with transitions and changes is to practice self-care and prioritize well-being. During times of change, it is important to take care of oneself both physically and mentally. This may involve engaging in activities that promote relaxation and stress relief, such as meditation, exercise, or spending time with loved ones. Prioritizing self-care can help individuals maintain a sense of balance and perspective during periods of transition, allowing them to better cope with the challenges that may arise.

Another important tip for dealing with transitions and changes is to stay flexible and open-minded. Change can be unpredictable, and it is important to be willing to adapt to new circumstances and embrace new opportunities. Approaching transitions with an open mind can help individuals see the potential for growth and development that may come with change. By remaining flexible and open-minded, individuals can navigate transitions more effectively and emerge from them with a greater sense of resilience and strength.

Communication is also a key aspect of managing transitions and changes. During periods of transition, it is important to communicate openly and effectively with others, whether they are colleagues, friends, or family members. Sharing thoughts and feelings with others can help individuals gain perspective and support during times of change. Additionally, seeking feedback and advice from others can help individuals consider different perspectives and approaches to managing transitions. By communicating openly and effectively with others, individuals can build stronger relationships and navigate transitions more effectively.

Setting goals and creating a plan can also be helpful in managing transitions and changes. During times of transition, it can be easy to feel overwhelmed and uncertain about the future. By setting clear goals and creating a plan for navigating the transition, individuals can establish a sense of direction and purpose. This can help individuals stay focused and motivated during periods of change, leading to greater clarity and confidence in managing transitions. By setting goals and creating a plan, individuals can approach transitions with a sense of purpose and intentionality, helping them navigate change more effectively.

It is also important to practice self-reflection and self-awareness during periods of transition. Taking time to reflect on one's thoughts, feelings, and reactions to change can help individuals gain insight into their coping mechanisms and emotional responses. By practicing self-reflection and self-awareness, individuals can better understand their strengths and weaknesses, allowing them to develop strategies for managing transitions more effectively. This can also help individuals identify areas for growth and improvement, leading to greater personal development and resilience in the face of change.

In short, seeking support from others can be a valuable resource for managing transitions and changes. During times of transition, it is important to reach out to friends, family members, mentors, or counselors for support and guidance. Building a strong support network can help individuals feel less isolated and alone during periods of change, providing them with emotional support and practical advice as they navigate transitions. Seeking support from others can also help individuals gain new perspectives and insights, leading to greater resilience and adaptability in managing transitions. By seeking support from others, individuals can build stronger relationships and tap into valuable resources for managing change effectively. By practicing self-care, staying flexible and open-minded, communicating effectively, setting goals and creating a plan, practicing self-reflection and self-awareness, and seeking support from others, individuals can develop the skills and strategies needed to manage transitions with resilience and grace. By implementing these tips, individuals can approach transitions with confidence and optimism, knowing that they have the tools and resources to navigate change effectively.

- How to handle challenging situations with grace

Life is full of unexpected challenges and difficult situations that can test our patience and resilience. It is important to be able to handle these challenges with grace and poise in order to maintain our mental and emotional well-being. Whether it is dealing with a difficult coworker, navigating a conflict with a friend, or facing a personal crisis, there are strategies that can help us navigate these challenging situations with grace.

One of the key components of handling challenging situations with grace is maintaining a positive attitude. This can be easier said than done, especially when faced with difficult circumstances. However, maintaining a positive outlook can help us approach the situation with a clear mind and avoid making decisions based on anger or frustration. Practicing gratitude and focusing on the good in our lives can help shift our mindset and enable us to tackle challenges with grace.

Another important aspect of handling challenging situations with grace is effective communication. Clear and respectful communication is essential in navigating difficult situations, whether it is expressing our feelings to a difficult coworker or discussing a conflict with a friend. It is important to listen actively, choose our words carefully, and communicate our thoughts and emotions honestly and tactfully. Effective communication can help prevent misunderstandings and conflicts from escalating, and ultimately lead to a more positive resolution.

In addition to maintaining a positive attitude and practicing effective communication, it is also important to practice self-care in order to handle challenging situations with grace. Taking care of our physical and mental well-being is essential in times of stress and adversity. This can include getting enough sleep, eating healthy, exercising regularly, and engaging in activities that bring us joy and relaxation. Self-care can help us maintain our resilience and ability to cope with difficult situations, allowing us to approach challenges with a sense of calm and grace.

Seeking support from trusted friends, family members, or professional counselors can also be beneficial in navigating challenging situations with grace. Talking to someone we trust about our feelings and experiences can provide us with valuable perspective and insight, as well as emotional support and encouragement. Seeking support can help us feel less alone in facing challenges and can help us gain the strength and resilience needed to handle difficult situations with grace.

Ultimately, handling challenging situations with grace is a skill that can be cultivated and developed over time. By maintaining a positive attitude, practicing effective communication, prioritizing self-care, and seeking support when needed, we can navigate difficult circumstances with grace and poise. While it may not always be easy, handling challenging situations with grace can lead to greater resilience, emotional well-being, and personal growth. By approaching challenges with grace and a positive mindset, we can overcome obstacles with strength and dignity, and emerge stronger and more resilient in the face of adversity.

Chapter 17: Building a Support Network

- Importance of seeking support and guidance from others

Seeking support and guidance from others is a vital aspect of personal and professional growth. It is important to recognize that no one can navigate life's challenges alone, and there is immense value in reaching out to others for assistance and advice. Whether it is seeking guidance from a mentor in the workplace, confiding in a friend during a difficult time, or seeking therapy to address emotional struggles, seeking support from others can provide invaluable insights and assistance in navigating life's complexities.

One of the key benefits of seeking support and guidance from others is the opportunity to gain new perspectives and insights. By engaging with individuals who have different backgrounds, experiences, and perspectives, we can expand our own understanding and challenge our assumptions. This can be particularly valuable in a professional setting, where seeking guidance from more experienced colleagues can help us navigate complex challenges and make informed decisions. In seeking support from others, we open ourselves up to new ideas and ways of thinking that can help us approach problems in a more creative and effective manner.

Additionally, seeking support and guidance from others can help us build and strengthen important relationships. By reaching out to others for assistance, we demonstrate vulnerability and trust, which can foster deeper connections with those around us. This can be particularly important in times of crisis or difficulty, as the support of others can provide emotional reassurance and validation. In seeking support from friends, family, or colleagues, we show that we value their input and trust their judgment, which can help to solidify bonds and nurture mutual respect.

Furthermore, seeking support and guidance from others can enhance our own personal development and self-awareness. By engaging with others who can provide constructive feedback and guidance, we can identify areas for growth and improvement. This can be particularly valuable in a professional setting, where seeking mentorship from more experienced individuals can help us develop our skills and reach our full potential. By seeking support from others, we open ourselves up to learning opportunities and can gain valuable feedback that can help us improve and refine our abilities.

In addition to the personal and professional benefits of seeking support and guidance from others, there is also a strong psychological benefit to reaching out for help. Research has shown that social support can have a positive impact on mental health and well-being, reducing feelings of isolation and loneliness. By seeking support from friends, family, or mental health professionals, we can access a safe space to express our emotions and work through our struggles. This can be particularly important during times of stress or difficulty, as having a support network can provide a sense of comfort and security. Whether in a personal or professional context, reaching out for assistance can provide valuable insights, build important relationships, enhance personal development, and support our mental well-being. By recognizing the value of seeking support from others, we can cultivate a stronger sense of resilience, adaptability, and connection in our lives. So, let us not hesitate to lean on others for support and guidance when needed, for it is through these connections that we can truly thrive and grow.

- Tips for finding support groups and resources

Support groups and resources play a crucial role in providing individuals with the necessary tools and assistance to navigate challenging situations and overcome obstacles in their lives. Whether facing a mental health issue, a chronic illness, addiction, or a major life transition, having access to a supportive community can make a significant difference in one's journey towards healing and growth. In this article, we will explore some tips for finding support groups and resources that are tailored to your specific needs and circumstances.

The first step in finding a support group or resource is to identify what specific challenges or issues you are facing and what type of support you are looking for. Are you seeking emotional support, practical advice, or simply a sense of community with others who can relate to your experiences. By clearly defining your needs and goals, you can narrow down your search and focus on finding a group or resource that aligns with your specific requirements.

One of the most common ways to find support groups and resources is through online research. There are numerous websites and online directories that provide information on a wide range of support groups, including those focused on mental health, addiction recovery, chronic illness, grief, and more. By using search engines and specialized websites, you can easily locate support groups in your area or ones that meet virtually. These online platforms also often provide details on meeting times, formats, and contact information for group leaders or facilitators.

In addition to online resources, seeking referrals from healthcare professionals, therapists, counselors, or community organizations can be a valuable way to find support groups and resources that are reputable and effective. These professionals often have knowledge of local support groups and can provide recommendations based on your specific needs and circumstances. By reaching out to trusted individuals in your network, you can access a wealth of information and connections to support groups that may not be readily available through online searches.

Attending community events, workshops, or conferences related to your specific needs can also be a productive way to connect with support groups and resources. These gatherings often feature presentations, discussions, and networking opportunities that can expose you to a variety of support options and introduce you to individuals who share similar experiences. By actively engaging in these events and reaching out to other attendees, you can expand your support network and gain valuable insights into available resources.

When considering joining a support group, it is essential to evaluate the group's structure, format, and approach to ensure that it aligns with your needs and preferences. Some support groups may follow a formalized curriculum or therapy-based model, while others may be more informal and peer-led. It's important to consider factors such as group size, frequency of meetings, confidentiality policies, and the focus of discussions when selecting a group to join.

Once you have identified a support group or resource that resonates with you, it is crucial to actively participate and engage with the group members. Building relationships with others who share similar experiences can provide a sense of belonging and validation, as well as opportunities for mutual support and encouragement. By sharing your own story, listening to others, offering advice, and asking for help when needed, you can help create a supportive and nurturing environment within the group. By utilizing online resources, seeking referrals from professionals, attending community events, and actively participating in support groups, you can connect with a supportive community that can provide you with the tools, encouragement, and understanding you need to navigate life's challenges. Remember that you are not alone in your journey, and there are resources and individuals ready to support you along the way.

- How to take care of yourself while caring for a child with ADHD

Caring for a child with ADHD can be a challenging and overwhelming experience for parents and caregivers. It's important to remember that taking care of yourself is just as important as taking care of your child. In order to provide the best care for your child, you must first prioritize your own physical and mental well-being. Self-care is not selfish, it is necessary in order to be able to effectively support your child.

One of the most important things you can do to take care of yourself while caring for a child with ADHD is to establish a solid support system. This can include family members, friends, therapists, support groups, or other caregivers who can offer emotional support, advice, and assistance when needed. It's important to reach out and ask for help when you need it, and not try to handle everything on your own. Remember, it's okay to not be perfect, and it's okay to ask for help.

Another key aspect of self-care is maintaining a healthy lifestyle. This includes getting enough sleep, eating a balanced diet, exercising regularly, and managing stress. These basic self-care practices can help you stay physically and mentally healthy, and better equipped to handle the challenges of caring for a child with ADHD. It's also important to make time for yourself and prioritize activities that bring you joy and relaxation, whether that's reading a book, going for a walk, or spending time with friends.

In addition to taking care of your physical health, it's also important to prioritize your mental health. Caring for a child with ADHD can be emotionally draining, so it's important to find healthy ways to cope with stress and prevent burnout. This may include seeking therapy or counseling, practicing mindfulness or meditation, or engaging in activities that help you relax and recharge. Remember, you can't pour from an empty cup, so taking care of your own mental health is crucial in order to be able to provide adequate care for your child.

It's also important to educate yourself about ADHD and learn effective strategies for managing your child's symptoms. This may involve working closely with your child's healthcare provider, attending parenting classes or workshops, or joining support groups for parents of children with ADHD. By arming yourself with knowledge and resources, you can feel empowered and better equipped to support your child in a way that is effective and sustainable. Remember, you are not alone in this journey, and there are resources and support available to help you navigate the challenges of caring for a child with ADHD. Remember to prioritize your physical and mental well-being, establish a solid support system, maintain a healthy lifestyle, and educate yourself about ADHD. By taking care of yourself, you can better support your child and create a more positive and nurturing environment for them to thrive. Remember, self-care is not selfish, it is necessary in order to be the best caregiver you can be.

Chapter 18: Celebrating Progress and Achievements

- Importance of recognizing and celebrating small victories

When we accomplish a task, no matter how small, it is important to take a moment to acknowledge and celebrate that achievement. This positive reinforcement not only boosts our self-esteem and confidence, but also inspires us to continue working towards our goals. By recognizing and celebrating small victories, we are able to stay motivated, focused, and driven to achieve even bigger successes in the future.

One of the main reasons why it is important to recognize and celebrate small victories is because it helps to build a positive mindset. By acknowledging our accomplishments, no matter how small they may seem, we are reinforcing the idea that we are capable of achieving our goals. This positive reinforcement can help to shift our perspective from focusing on our failures and shortcomings to recognizing our strengths and successes. When we have a positive mindset, we are better able to overcome obstacles and setbacks, and approach challenges with a sense of confidence and optimism.

In addition to building a positive mindset, recognizing and celebrating small victories also helps to boost our self-esteem and confidence. When we achieve a goal, no matter how small, it is important to acknowledge our hard work and effort that went into accomplishing that task. By celebrating our achievements, we are reinforcing the belief that we are capable of success and that our efforts are paying off. This positive reinforcement can help to improve our self-esteem and confidence, enabling us to tackle even greater challenges and goals with a sense of self-assurance and determination.

Furthermore, recognizing and celebrating small victories can help to increase our motivation and focus. When we take the time to acknowledge and celebrate our achievements, we are reinforcing the idea that our hard work and efforts are worthwhile. This positive reinforcement can help to keep us motivated and focused on our goals, even when faced with obstacles and challenges. By recognizing and celebrating small victories, we are able to maintain a sense of momentum and progress, which can help to keep us on track and moving forward towards our larger goals.

Another important reason why it is essential to recognize and celebrate small victories is that it can help to cultivate a sense of gratitude and appreciation. By taking the time to acknowledge our accomplishments, we are expressing gratitude for our efforts and the progress we have made. This sense of gratitude can help us to recognize the support and contributions of others, as well as our own capabilities and strengths. By celebrating our achievements, we are also taking the time to appreciate the journey and the process of achieving our goals, rather than just focusing on the end result. By building a positive mindset, boosting our self-esteem and confidence, increasing our motivation and focus, and cultivating a sense of gratitude and appreciation, we are able to stay motivated, resilient, and driven towards achieving our goals. So, the next time you accomplish a task, no matter how small, take a moment to acknowledge and celebrate that achievement.

- Strategies for boosting confidence and motivation

Confidence and motivation are crucial factors in achieving success in any aspect of life. Whether it be in academic pursuits, professional endeavors, or personal goals, having a strong sense of self-assurance and drive can make all the difference in overcoming challenges and reaching one's full potential. However, boosting confidence and motivation is not always easy, especially when faced with setbacks or obstacles. In this discussion, we will explore various strategies that can help individuals cultivate a more positive mindset and strengthen their belief in themselves.

One of the most effective ways to boost confidence and motivation is through setting clear and achievable goals. By defining specific objectives and breaking them down into manageable steps, individuals can create a roadmap for success that provides direction and a sense of purpose. Setting realistic expectations and celebrating small victories along the way can also help build confidence and keep motivation levels high. Additionally, establishing a support system of friends, family, or mentors who can provide encouragement and guidance can further bolster one's self-assurance and drive.

Another key strategy for boosting confidence and motivation is by practicing self-care and maintaining a healthy lifestyle. Taking care of one's physical and mental well-being can have a significant impact on one's overall outlook and sense of self-worth. Engaging in regular exercise, getting an adequate amount of sleep, and eating a balanced diet can help improve energy levels and mood, which can in turn boost confidence and motivation. Practicing mindfulness and relaxation techniques, such as meditation or deep breathing exercises, can also help reduce stress and increase mental clarity, further fostering a positive mindset.

Additionally, developing a growth mindset can be instrumental in boosting confidence and motivation. A growth mindset is the belief that abilities and intelligence can be developed through dedication and hard work, rather than being fixed traits. By reframing challenges as opportunities for growth and learning, individuals can cultivate a more resilient and optimistic attitude towards setbacks and failures. Embracing a growth mindset can also help individuals overcome self-doubt and fear of failure, enabling them to take risks and pursue new opportunities with confidence and enthusiasm.

Furthermore, seeking out opportunities for personal and professional development can help individuals boost their confidence and motivation. Whether it be through formal education, training programs, or networking events, investing in oneself and acquiring new skills can bolster one's sense of competence and capability. Engaging in activities that align with one's passions and interests can also enhance motivation levels and provide a sense of fulfillment. By continuously seeking out opportunities for growth and self-improvement, individuals can maintain a positive and proactive attitude towards their goals and aspirations. By setting clear goals, practicing self-care, developing a growth mindset, and seeking out opportunities for development, individuals can cultivate a more positive and resilient mindset that empowers them to overcome challenges and achieve their full potential. By implementing these strategies and incorporating them into daily routines, individuals can build the confidence and motivation needed to thrive in all aspects of life.

- Tips for staying positive and hopeful

Staying positive and hopeful in the face of life's challenges can be a difficult task, but it is essential for maintaining a healthy mindset and outlook on life. While it is normal to experience moments of doubt and negativity, there are several strategies that can help you cultivate a more positive and hopeful attitude. In this article, we will discuss some tips for staying positive and hopeful, even when things may seem bleak.

One of the most important tips for staying positive and hopeful is to practice gratitude on a daily basis. Taking the time to reflect on the things in your life that you are grateful for can help shift your focus from what you lack to what you have. This can help you appreciate the positive aspects of your life and improve your overall mood. Keeping a gratitude journal can be a helpful tool for cultivating a sense of gratitude and optimism.

Another important tip for staying positive and hopeful is to surround yourself with positive influences. This can include spending time with friends and family who uplift you, engaging in activities that bring you joy and fulfillment, and consuming positive and uplifting media. By surrounding yourself with positivity, you can help counteract negative thoughts and feelings and maintain a more hopeful outlook.

In addition to surrounding yourself with positive influences, it is important to practice self-care and self-compassion. Taking care of your physical, emotional, and mental well-being can help you better cope with stress and adversity. This can include getting enough sleep, eating a healthy diet, exercising regularly, and engaging in activities that bring you joy and relaxation. Practicing self-compassion can also help you be kinder to yourself and more forgiving of your perceived flaws and shortcomings.

Another important tip for staying positive and hopeful is to practice mindfulness and stay present in the moment. Mindfulness involves paying attention to your thoughts, feelings, and sensations in a non-judgmental way. By practicing mindfulness, you can learn to observe your thoughts and feelings without getting caught up in them, which can help reduce negative thinking patterns and increase your sense of peace and contentment. Staying present in the moment can also help you appreciate the beauty and joy that can be found in everyday experiences.

It is also helpful to set realistic goals and focus on progress rather than perfection. Setting realistic goals can help you stay motivated and focused, while also allowing for flexibility and self-compassion. Focusing on progress, rather than perfection, can help you celebrate your achievements and maintain a positive attitude, even when things may not go as planned. By setting realistic goals and focusing on progress, you can stay motivated and hopeful, even in the face of setbacks.

Lastly, it is important to seek support from others when you are struggling to stay positive and hopeful. Talking to friends, family, or a therapist can help you process your thoughts and feelings and gain a fresh perspective on your situation. Seeking support can also help you feel less alone in your struggles and provide you with encouragement and guidance to help you stay positive and hopeful. By practicing gratitude, surrounding yourself with positive influences, practicing self-care and self-compassion, staying present in the moment, setting realistic goals, and seeking support from others, you can cultivate a more positive and hopeful attitude, even in the face of life's challenges. Remember that it is normal to experience moments of doubt and negativity, but by implementing these tips, you can maintain a sense of optimism and hopefulness in all areas of your life.

Chapter 19: Looking Towards the Future

- Planning for the future of your child with ADHD

Attention deficit hyperactivity disorder (ADHD) is a neurodevelopmental disorder that affects individuals of all ages, but is particularly common in children. The symptoms of ADHD, which include inattention, hyperactivity, and impulsivity, can have a significant impact on a child's daily functioning, academic performance, and social relationships. As a parent of a child with ADHD, it is important to plan for your child's future in order to help them reach their full potential and thrive in all areas of their life.

One of the first steps in planning for the future of your child with ADHD is to educate yourself about the disorder and its impact on your child's development. Understanding the characteristics of ADHD, as well as the challenges and strengths associated with the disorder, can help you better support your child and advocate for their needs. It is also important to stay informed about the latest research and treatment options for ADHD, as new approaches and interventions continue to emerge that can benefit children with the disorder.

In addition to educating yourself about ADHD, it is essential to work closely with your child's healthcare providers, including physicians, therapists, and educators, to develop a comprehensive treatment plan that addresses your child's individual needs. This may include medication management, behavioral therapy, academic accommodations, and other supports that can help your child succeed in school, at home, and in social settings. By collaborating with a team of professionals who specialize in ADHD, you can ensure that your child receives the best possible care and support to reach their full potential.

As your child with ADHD grows and develops, it is important to start thinking about their future goals and aspirations. Encouraging your child to explore their interests, talents, and passions can help them discover their strengths and build self-confidence. It is also important to set realistic and achievable goals for your child, while providing them with the necessary support and guidance to work towards their objectives. By helping your child develop a positive self-image and a sense of agency, you can empower them to overcome challenges and pursue their dreams.

In addition to focusing on your child's individual strengths and interests, it is important to consider their unique needs and challenges when planning for their future. Children with ADHD may face obstacles in areas such as executive function, organization, time management, and social skills, which can impact their academic and career success. By providing your child with the tools and strategies they need to navigate these challenges, you can help them build resilience and adaptability in the face of adversity.

When thinking about your child's future, it is also important to consider the transition to adulthood and independence. Adolescents with ADHD may need additional support and guidance to navigate the challenges of transitioning to college, vocational training, or the workforce. By working with your child to develop practical skills such as time management, organization, and self-advocacy, you can help them build the confidence and independence they need to succeed in the adult world. By educating yourself about the disorder, collaborating with healthcare providers, empowering your child to pursue their interests and goals, and preparing them for the transition to adulthood, you can help your child thrive and reach their full potential. With the right support and guidance, children with ADHD can overcome challenges, build resilience, and achieve success in all areas of their life.

- Strategies for preparing for the teenage years

The teenage years can be a tumultuous time for both adolescents and their parents. The changes that occur during this period can be challenging to navigate, but with proper preparation and strategies in place, the transition can be smoother for everyone involved. In this article, we will discuss various strategies for preparing for the teenage years, including open communication, setting boundaries, building trust, and fostering independence.

One of the most important strategies for preparing for the teenage years is open communication. Adolescents are going through a time of significant physical, emotional, and cognitive development, and they may be experiencing a wide range of emotions and thoughts. It is crucial for parents to create an environment where their teenager feels comfortable expressing themselves and discussing their feelings. By fostering open communication, parents can gain insight into their teenager's thoughts and emotions, which can help strengthen their relationship and build trust.

Setting boundaries is another crucial strategy for preparing for the teenage years. While teenagers are seeking independence and autonomy, they still need guidance and structure to navigate the challenges of adolescence. Parents should establish clear and consistent boundaries that are age-appropriate and aligned with their family values. By setting boundaries, parents can help their teenager understand expectations and consequences and promote responsible behavior.

Building trust is essential for preparing for the teenage years. As teenagers navigate the complexities of adolescence, they may encounter difficult situations and decisions. It is essential for parents to trust their teenager and provide them with support and guidance when needed. By building trust, parents can show their teenager that they are there for them and can offer a safe and supportive environment for them to grow and develop.

Fostering independence is another important strategy for preparing for the teenage years. As teenagers strive for independence, parents should encourage their teenager to take on more responsibilities and make their own decisions. By fostering independence, parents can help their teenager develop essential life skills, such as problem-solving, decision-making, and self-regulation. This can help teenagers build confidence and prepare them for the challenges of adulthood. By implementing these strategies, parents can help their teenager navigate the challenges of adolescence and build a strong and supportive relationship. The teenage years may be challenging, but with proper preparation and strategies in place, both parents and teenagers can navigate this period with grace and understanding.

- Importance of setting long-term goals and aspirations

Setting long-term goals and aspirations is a crucial aspect of personal and professional development. It allows individuals to create a roadmap for their future, guiding their actions and decisions towards achieving their desired outcomes. Without clear long-term goals and aspirations, individuals may feel lost or uncertain about their future, leading to a lack of motivation and fulfillment in their lives.

One of the key benefits of setting long-term goals and aspirations is that it helps individuals focus their efforts and resources on activities that are aligned with their values and priorities. By having a clear vision of what they want to achieve in the future, individuals can make strategic decisions that will bring them closer to their goals. This focus allows individuals to avoid distractions and time-wasting activities, leading to greater productivity and efficiency in their work and personal lives. In addition, setting long-term goals helps individuals prioritize their tasks and commitments, ensuring that they are working towards their desired outcomes consistently.

Moreover, setting long-term goals and aspirations provides individuals with a sense of purpose and direction in their lives. When individuals have a clear vision of what they want to achieve in the future, it gives them a reason to wake up every morning and work towards their goals. By setting long-term goals and aspirations, individuals can find meaning and fulfillment in their lives, leading to greater satisfaction and joy.

Furthermore, setting long-term goals and aspirations allows individuals to measure their progress and track their achievements over time. By breaking down long-term goals into smaller, manageable tasks and milestones, individuals can monitor their progress and celebrate their successes along the way. This sense of accomplishment and progress can boost individuals' confidence and self-esteem, motivating them to continue working towards their long-term goals. Additionally, tracking progress towards long-term goals can help individuals identify areas for improvement and make adjustments to their plans as needed, ensuring that they stay on track and reach their desired outcomes.

In addition, setting long-term goals and aspirations can lead to increased self-discipline and resilience. Achieving long-term goals requires dedication, perseverance, and the ability to overcome obstacles and challenges along the way. By setting ambitious goals that require sustained effort and commitment, individuals can develop important skills such as time management, prioritization, and problem-solving. These skills are essential for personal and professional success, as they enable individuals to navigate complex situations and achieve their desired outcomes. Moreover, working towards long-term goals can build resilience and mental toughness, as individuals learn to adapt to change and overcome setbacks in pursuit of their aspirations. It provides individuals with a sense of purpose and direction, helps them focus their efforts and resources on activities that align with their values and priorities, and allows them to measure their progress and track their achievements over time. Additionally, pursuing long-term goals can lead to increased self-discipline, resilience, and the development of important skills that are essential for personal and professional success. By setting clear long-term goals and aspirations, individuals can create a roadmap for their future and work towards achieving their desired outcomes, leading to greater satisfaction and fulfillment in their lives.

Chapter 20: Conclusion

- Recap of key parenting strategies for children with ADHD

Attention-deficit/hyperactivity disorder (ADHD) is a neurodevelopmental disorder that affects many children and can present challenges for both the child and their parents. In order to effectively manage the symptoms of ADHD and help children thrive, it is important for parents to employ key parenting strategies. These strategies can help improve behavior, academic performance, and overall well-being for children with ADHD. In this recap, we will explore some of the key parenting strategies that have been shown to be effective in supporting children with ADHD.

One of the most important strategies for parents of children with ADHD is to establish a structured routine. Children with ADHD often struggle with organizing their time and tasks, so having a predictable routine can help provide a sense of security and stability. Parents should create a daily schedule that includes specific times for meals, homework, chores, and bedtime. It can also be helpful to use visual aids, such as a calendar or whiteboard, to help children understand and follow the routine.

Another important strategy for parents of children with ADHD is to provide clear and consistent expectations. Children with ADHD may have difficulty understanding and remembering rules, so it is important for parents to be clear and consistent in their expectations. Parents should clearly communicate the rules and consequences for breaking them, and follow through with consequences when necessary. It can also be helpful to provide positive reinforcement for good behavior, such as praise or rewards, to help motivate children to follow the rules.

In addition to providing structure and clear expectations, parents of children with ADHD should also focus on developing and reinforcing positive behaviors. Children with ADHD may struggle with impulsivity and hyperactivity, so it is important for parents to help them learn alternative, more positive ways of behaving. Parents can do this by using techniques such as positive reinforcement, modeling, and role-playing. For example, parents can praise and reward children for following the rules, and demonstrate appropriate behavior for them to emulate.

Another key strategy for parents of children with ADHD is to create a supportive environment. Children with ADHD may have difficulty focusing and staying organized, so it is important for parents to create a space that is conducive to their learning and development. This may include minimizing distractions, providing organizational tools such as bins or folders, and creating a quiet and calm environment for homework and study time. Parents should also be supportive and empathetic towards their child, and work to build a strong and positive relationship with them.

To recapitulate, it is important for parents of children with ADHD to educate themselves about the disorder and seek support from professionals. ADHD is a complex condition that can manifest in different ways for each child, so it is important for parents to educate themselves about the symptoms, treatment options, and strategies for managing the disorder. Parents should work closely with teachers, doctors, and therapists to create a comprehensive treatment plan that addresses the specific needs of their child. By arming themselves with knowledge and seeking support from professionals, parents can better support their child with ADHD and help them thrive in all aspects of their life. By taking a proactive and informed approach to parenting, parents can help their child with ADHD navigate the challenges of the disorder and reach their full potential. Remember, every child is unique and may respond differently to various strategies, so it is important for parents to be flexible and patient as they work to find what works best for their child. With the right support and guidance, children with ADHD can thrive and succeed in all areas of their life.

- Encouragement to continue supporting and nurturing children with ADHD

Attention-deficit/hyperactivity disorder (ADHD) is a neurodevelopmental disorder that affects millions of children worldwide. It is characterized by symptoms of inattention, impulsivity, and hyperactivity that can make everyday tasks and interactions more challenging for affected individuals. Despite the challenges that come with managing ADHD, it is important for parents, teachers, and other caregivers to continue supporting and nurturing children with this disorder.

One of the key reasons why it is crucial to continue supporting children with ADHD is to help them reach their full potential. Children with ADHD often struggle with tasks that require sustained attention and executive functioning skills, which can impact their academic performance and social relationships. By providing these children with the necessary support and resources, we can help them develop coping strategies and skills to navigate their challenges more effectively. This can ultimately lead to improved academic outcomes, greater self-confidence, and stronger interpersonal relationships.

Additionally, by continuing to support children with ADHD, we can help reduce the stigma and misconceptions surrounding this disorder. Many people mistakenly believe that ADHD is simply a result of laziness or lack of discipline, when in fact it is a complex neurobiological condition that requires understanding and empathy. By educating others about the realities of ADHD and advocating for evidence-based interventions, we can help create a more inclusive and supportive environment for individuals with this disorder.

Furthermore, supporting children with ADHD can also benefit society as a whole. Research has shown that individuals with ADHD are often creative, innovative, and have unique perspectives that can contribute positively to various industries and fields. By nurturing these qualities and helping children with ADHD build on their strengths, we can help unleash their full potential and foster a more diverse and dynamic workforce in the future.

In order to effectively support and nurture children with ADHD, it is important to take a multi-faceted approach that addresses their unique needs and challenges. This may include implementing behavioral interventions, providing academic accommodations, and offering psychological support. It is also crucial to work closely with parents, teachers, and healthcare professionals to create a supportive and collaborative network that can help children with ADHD thrive.

Parents play a particularly important role in supporting their children with ADHD. By providing love, understanding, and consistent structure at home, parents can help their children build resilience and develop self-regulation skills. It is also important for parents to educate themselves about ADHD and stay informed about the latest research and treatment options. By becoming advocates for their children and working closely with their healthcare providers, parents can help ensure that their children receive the best possible care and support.

Teachers and other educational professionals also play a critical role in supporting children with ADHD. By creating a supportive and inclusive learning environment, teachers can help children with ADHD thrive academically and socially. This may involve implementing classroom accommodations, providing targeted interventions, and fostering a positive and encouraging atmosphere. It is also important for teachers to collaborate with parents and healthcare professionals to create a coordinated approach to supporting children with ADHD. By providing love, understanding, and evidence-based interventions, we can help these children reach their full potential and thrive in all areas of their lives. Together, we can help reduce the stigma surrounding ADHD, promote a more inclusive society, and foster a brighter future for children with this disorder. Let us continue to advocate for the needs of children with ADHD and work together to create a more supportive and understanding environment for all individuals affected by this disorder.

- Importance of seeking help and staying committed to your child's well-being.

As parents, one of the most important responsibilities we have is to ensure the well-being and success of our children. This means not only providing for their physical needs, but also supporting their emotional and mental health. It is crucial that we are proactive in seeking help and staying committed to our child's well-being, as this can have a profound impact on their overall development and happiness.

Seeking help for your child's well-being is not a sign of weakness, but rather a sign of strength and love. It takes courage to acknowledge when your child may be struggling and to reach out for support. By seeking help, you are showing your child that you care about their well-being and are willing to do whatever it takes to help them thrive. Whether it be seeking counseling, therapy, or medical treatment, getting the right support can make a world of difference for your child's mental and emotional health.

Staying committed to your child's well-being means being consistent and persistent in your efforts to support them. Building a strong foundation of trust and communication with your child is essential in fostering a healthy and positive relationship. This means actively listening to your child, validating their feelings, and providing a safe and nurturing environment for them to express themselves. It also means being aware of any warning signs or red flags that may indicate your child is struggling and taking appropriate action to address these issues.

Parenting is a journey that requires constant learning and adaptation. It is important to educate yourself about child development, mental health, and effective parenting strategies in order to best support your child's well-being. This may involve attending parenting classes, reading books, or seeking guidance from professionals. Remember, you are not alone in this journey. There are numerous resources and support networks available to help you navigate the challenges of parenting and ensure the well-being of your child.

In addition to seeking help and staying committed to your child's well-being, it is also important to prioritize self-care as a parent. Taking care of yourself is essential in order to effectively care for your child. This means getting enough rest, engaging in activities that bring you joy and relaxation, and seeking support from friends and family when needed. Remember, you are a role model for your child and by prioritizing your own well-being, you are teaching them the importance of self-care and emotional resilience. By being proactive in addressing your child's emotional and mental health needs, you are setting them up for a lifetime of success and happiness. Remember, it is okay to ask for help and to prioritize your child's well-being above all else. Together, we can create a brighter future for our children and help them reach their full potential.